ENCOUNTERS WITH GOD

10 Women, 10 Testimonies

COMPILED BY SHARON FINNEY

Rose of Sharon Publishing

Copyright © 2020
SHARON FINNEY
ENCOUNTERS WITH GOD
10 Women, 10 Testimonies
All rights reserved.

No part of this publication may be reproduced, distributed, or transmitted in any form or by any means, including photocopying, recording, or other electronic or mechanical methods, without the prior written permission of the publisher, except in the case of brief quotations embodied in critical reviews and certain other non-commercial uses permitted by copyright law.

SHARON FINNEY

Printed in the United States of America
First Printing 2020
First Edition 2020

ISBN: 979-8683158699

10 9 8 7 6 5 4 3 2 1

Scriptures marked NIV are taken from the NEW INTERNATIONAL VERSION (NIV): Scripture taken from THE HOLY BIBLE, NEW INTERNATIONAL VERSION ®. Copyright© 1973, 1978, 1984, 2011 by Biblica, Inc.™. Used by permission of Zondervan.
Scriptures marked ESV are taken from the THE HOLY BIBLE, ENGLISH STANDARD VERSION (ESV): Scriptures taken from THE HOLY BIBLE, ENGLISH STANDARD VERSION ® Copyright© 2001 by Crossway, a publishing ministry of Good News Publishers. Used by permission.
Scriptures marked KJV are taken from the KING JAMES VERSION (KJV): KING JAMES VERSION, public domain.

This book is dedicated to my husband Lewis and our children who lovingly support every idea that crosses my mind. I also want to acknowledge everyone who had a role in my relationship with Christ including my godmother who not only provides inspiration in countless ways, but for being that extra set of eyes on Encounters with God. On this journey, I have come to know many pastors, ministry leaders, and people who truly have a heart for God. Every encounter has served a great purpose. I trust that my late parents and grandparents are smiling down from heaven because of the seeds planted many years ago.

To the co-authors, April, Ayeshia, Deblen, Dileika, Donna, Marva, Sherae, Tamica, and Vernetta; I thank you for your trust, patience, and dedication. You have shared your heart(s) in writing and taken obedience to another level. I got chills watching you work these past few months, and I pray the relationships last a lifetime.

Table of Contents

INTRODUCTION..*i*

FOREWORD.. *iii*

1. BECAUSE GOD SAID IT 1

   Sharon Finney

2. DELAYED BUT NOT DENIED......................................15

   Tamica R. Simon

3. DON'T RUN! WALK!..25

   Vernetta Dunbar

4. WON'T HE DO IT 37

   April Joy Bowden

5. HEAR HIS VOICE AND OBEY 49

   Deblen B. Edge

6. MY STORY; MY TESTIMONY 61

   Rev. Marva J. Cumberbatch Wilson

7. BRIDGING GAPS: GOD'S GIFT TO ME 73

   Donna "DeeDee" Suttles

8. DANCING FOR AN AUDIENCE OF ONE 85

   Dileika Wilson-Ballard

9. SURRENDER 95
    Ayeshia Duru
10. YOU ARE ENOUGH 107
    Sherae D. Bell
11. SWEET MAGNOLIA'S BIBLE 117
    Sharon Finney
MEET THE VISIONARY AUTHOR 119
    SHARON FINNEY
MEET THE COAUTHORS 121
    APRIL JOY BOWDEN 121
    AYESHIA DURU 123
    DEBLEN B. EDGE 125
    DILEIKA WILSON-BALLARD 127
    DONNA SUTTLES 129
    MARVA J. CUMBERBATCH WILSON 131
    SHERAE D. BELL... 133
    TAMICA R. SIMON... 135
    VERNETTA DUNBAR 137

INTRODUCTION

God is awesome in all His ways. While adjusting to a new work routine, I recognized the abundance of time gained from not enduring a daily commute. I had time to think and my mind was clear. Even with some unfortunate occurrences in recent months, I found myself drawing nearer to God with great fervor. Many long for such experiences, and for me, it has been refreshing to know God hears my every thought. I already knew he heard me, but seeing things manifest just as He spoke them to me in 2007 caused a quickening in my spirit.

In my quiet time, I heard "An encounter with God" followed by the names of women to contact. A small part of me felt reluctant about saying, "Hey, what does this mean to you?", or "Is this something you could write about?" Perhaps fear of rejection played a role in my hesitation. But THANKS BE TO GOD, many women were affirmative in their responses. For some, the reply

INTRODUCTION

came without hesitation, asking me how many words and when I would need it by. Others needed time to see what it would entail. Because I wasn't specific when presenting the initial question, I had to finally share that God was leading me to a book project.

I can't begin to thank these nine phenomenal women enough for trusting me in this. I didn't have all the answers, but I knew it would require discipline and research to compile and publish individual testimonies and very private moments that they had with our heavenly Father. As we worked virtually side-by-side during a worldwide pandemic, we have demonstrated camaraderie in a blessed way.

It is my prayer that our book is an encouragement for some and a step closer to God for others. May God richly bless all supporters of this endeavor as *Encounters with God* is meaningless without you!

FOREWORD

It's not an accident or coincidence when Jesus selected a group of men with wide and various backgrounds, to partner with Him in sharing the greatest story ever told; a story that touched and changed the lives of many. In like manner nine women have partnered with author Sharon M. Finney to share their powerful, life-changing stories. Encounters with God will take you on a journey that will touch your heart, mind, and soul while showing God's grace and love during life's challenging moments. From the beginning, readers will be in awe and inspired by these untold experiences of these amazing women. Thank you, ladies, for allowing the Lord to use you in such a revealing way! May His grace and love be with you now and always.

Pastor Lewis H. Finney

1. BECAUSE GOD SAID IT

SHARON FINNEY

God Spared Me

Why am I here? What is my purpose? I came into the world abruptly, born prematurely as mom carried me for roughly five and a half months. My birth weight was only 2 pounds 11 ounces, so I remained in the NICU for six weeks working on gaining weight and strength. During this period, my parents could not even hold me. Mom returned home to care for my brother as dad continued doing his duties as a soldier. They were a young couple and getting to the hospital proved challenging, but they received consistent reports from my godmother who worked at the hospital. The nurses were good about keeping them informed as well. My dad often joked about how active I was in the incubator. Based on his stories I would somehow move about just enough to end up on one side of the bassinet while my diaper was on the other. I guess I wanted to prove how strong I was so I could come home to my family! My brother was only 8 months old, an infant himself when our mom went into labor with me. If I had not been in such a hurry, we would be a year apart. But because I showed up early, mom endured a few jokes from her friends through the years.

When I was around 6 years old, I learned our family was growing. Finally, I won't be the baby anymore. I was excited about having a younger sibling! Much to our surprise, mom gave birth to another premature daughter who weighed even less than I did. She was so small and not strong enough to survive. Her life ended on the same day of her birth. As if that weren't painful enough, mom and dad went through the same experience the following year with another baby girl. It breaks my heart knowing both of my baby sisters lived less than a day. I recall speaking with mom briefly about it, asking what happened since the babies died. She explained that they went to heaven, so I accepted that thought and didn't mention it again. I often wondered how my parents made it through those painful moments. Then, as I got older, I wondered why my life was spared. I still have their birth certificates.

1. BECAUSE GOD SAID IT

From time to time, I'll open the folder, read them and tuck them away. Why was I the survivor out of three premature baby girls born to the same parents? This is a burden I would carry into adulthood.

In my walk with Christ, I have learned the importance of fulfilling my destiny according to God's will and not mine. I know it sounds cliché, but God kept me here for a reason. Marla and Monique's lives on earth were for less than a day and we started with the same circumstances. Though I will never fully understand the why behind our family losing them, I must put to good use every day that I am granted in this earthly vessel.

"...he who began a good work in you will carry it on to completion until the day of Christ Jesus." (Philippians 1:6, NIV)

Planted

My parents decided to have me baptized when I was six months old. I still have my *certificado de bautismo* and the many pictures of that special day. I was surrounded by my family members and my godparents. Mom and Dad grew up in differing cultures. He was born and raised in the U.S., and she was born and raised in Panama. The irony is that both were raised in Methodist churches, so quite naturally my baptism took place in *Iglesia Metodista*. Spanish is the official language of Panama, but my mother's household was bilingual, speaking Spanish and English. I was never fluent in Spanish, but I take pride in dropping a word or two in my conversations acknowledging my Panamanian heritage. That's evident as I described my baptism with the use of 'Spanglish'.

I'm thankful for my parents choosing to raise us in the knowledge of the Lord until we could decide for ourselves how we would live our own lives. They planted the seeds early on as the same was done for them. I know I was protected by the prayers of loved ones through the years until I'd make the decision to live my life in Christ, and what a journey this has been. God has a way of speaking to us even when we are not giving him our undivided attention. At least, this is what I experienced. I guess you can say I knew of God, but I didn't fully know God. Throughout my youth, I believed Jesus was real, but I thought you had to come a certain way to receive salvation. I hesitated to receive salvation because I needed to fix what I knew was wrong before coming to Christ. Somehow I missed the fact that I could come and receive the help that I so desperately needed. This way of thinking

1. BECAUSE GOD SAID IT

led to years of waiting, learning of the Lord, but not fully choosing to come to Christ.

Whenever I reflect on my spiritual growth and development, I immediately recall standing at the bus stop with my brother and some neighborhood kids dressed in our Sunday best. Like many other military families, we attended the post chapel. We rode the bus to Sunday School then our parents would later join us for worship service. In addition to chapel, we also spent time at church with our grandparents where they held membership for as long as I can remember. Since we relocated every two to three years, our chapel experiences would change, but the message was the same. We learned about the love of Jesus. Our Sunday School routine involved assembling with all age groups in the fellowship hall before attending classes. We'd sing *Into My Heart* before splitting up into smaller classes based on our age. I loved singing during our group fellowship, and because I had a very active imagination, I would find myself mentally processing the words to the song.

"Into my heart, into my heart, come into my heart, Lord Jesus;

Come in today, come in to stay, come into my heart, Lord Jesus!"

This song caused me to envision a big red heart, like a Valentine's day card opening and Jesus taking steps inside. Though I loved this song and what it meant, I did not act on accepting Jesus into my heart. Years were spent in Sunday School and various churches. Then there was Vacation Bible School which I enjoyed with my brothers and our cousins if they were visiting. Somehow, I still waited many years to accept Jesus into my heart. I am grateful that seeds were planted early on and that so many were praying for my safety and protection before I was saved.

Watered

Why did it take so long for my journey to develop? It's not like I wasn't exposed to church and the word of God. I had multiple opportunities to grow, and I understood what it all meant, yet the reluctance was still there. I graduated from college and actively served in the military. My experience as a soldier, took me to the Persian Gulf 5 ½ months after losing my father, my hero and favorite Army soldier. As we prepared to funeralize him, I KNEW I needed to change my life and accept Christ. I

1. BECAUSE GOD SAID IT

grew up learning about the love of Jesus and I knew God was real, but at this point, I still had not received salvation. Well, God had to fly me 7,525 miles away from home to Saudi Arabia for me to finally accept Jesus into my heart. While at the Port of Dammam awaiting equipment so our unit could set up, the opportunity presented itself. I was invited to bible study with one of my colleagues, a former classmate who was also in my battalion. This was about a week after arriving in Saudi Arabia. I reached a point in my life where I had to choose. Standing in what would soon become a war zone knowing I'd prepared my first will right before leaving home, my mind was all over the place. I was young and was not ready to think about death and dying. Somehow, being on foreign soil in an Army uniform led to my conversion experience. Though I sometimes question the timing, I know it all happened according to God's plan and at the best time for me. I know I was spared while making some reckless decisions during young adulthood. Sometimes I get annoyed by those actions, yet, the things I have been through are all a part of who I am. Every situation and circumstance that I survived speak to how powerful God is. Since receiving Christ as my Lord and savior, God's presence has taken on new meaning, I have learned to recognize that still small voice speaking to me. Sometimes it is soothing, while other encounters are downright uncomfortable! God meets me where I am and deals with me, especially when the flesh wants to act out, but the spirit knows better! Now and then an encounter would seemingly feel like I'm losing control. I don't mean this negatively, but more so in the form of submission. These are constant reminders that my life is in God's hands.

Increase

About fifteen years ago, I joined the dance ministry at my church. My daughter was eight years old and had already committed to dancing with the girl's group, but the ladies dance group was newly established. Most of us were mothers of the youth dance ministry, and since we were bringing our daughters anyway, it seemed to be a good way to keep busy. I also needed a fitness routine after leaving the military and straying away from exercise. I tried to believe I was advanced since I took ballet for two years during elementary school. (We won't speak on that one adult ballet class that I tried). I welcomed this seemingly fun way to stay in shape. Because I was in band throughout high school and college, I understood the fine details about learning routines and being on one accord with fellow members, but this background was not quite like what was

1. BECAUSE GOD SAID IT

to come. Joining the women's dance ministry taught another form of discipline and structure, perfecting movements while focused on the word of God. Little did I know how dance would contribute to my spiritual growth and development.

The Spirit of the Sovereign Lord is on me... (Isaiah 61:1, NIV)

A few months after dancing in conjunction with the teen and youth groups, Ladies of Grace began rehearsing to dance alone. We would soon minister to the 23rd Psalm. Our director chose the version performed by Jeff Majors, a known harpist in the gospel music industry. This rendition was beautiful incorporating the harp and the voice of a soloist for most of the song. We worked hard rehearsing and deciding what movements would go best with the words. We wanted to fully articulate that which was described in those six verses of scripture. The sounds of the harp captivated us as we started each rehearsal of this dance. It almost felt like the words were being spoken from the heavens. The 23rd Psalm was familiar to all of us, yet, we carefully listened to every word as each verse was so eloquently expressed to the flowing sound of this and other stringed instruments. We rehearsed countless times, perfecting the moves and ensuring what we executed somehow coincided with the words in the verses. We wore black palazzo pants that resembled a skirt at first glance. Our tops were white with sleeves that flared at the wrist giving an angelic look. Each dancer held in her hands a white, rectangular scarf which was incorporated into the movements.

The day we were to perform, or minister this dance, we had our usual time of prayer together after putting on our praise garments. We stood near the entrance patiently waiting for our cue. As the sound technicians got our music ready, we lined up in the aisle to gracefully assume our positions. The lights went down, the tech hit play, and our song encamped the sanctuary. By the time the instrumental portion was complete, the tone was already set. The sound of the shofar seconds into the introduction signified our procession and made a bold statement. The atmosphere caused worshippers to quiet their hearts and feel the message through song and dance. We were all in place as these words, "The Lord is my Shepherd" filled the sanctuary. I was at the front, so I could not see expressions or movements of the other ladies, though I tried to glance occasionally using my peripheral vision. Suddenly, the nervousness I remember from ballet came back, then the confidence that I gained marching in the university band

1. BECAUSE GOD SAID IT

before packed stadium crowds reminded me that perfect practice makes perfect performance. I knew how intense our practices were and that all of us were ready. What I did not anticipate was how the verses of this passage would impact me while ministering to the people of God.

As we simulated walking through the valley, my feet felt as though they weren't even touching the floor. Each movement was effortless. We wrapped the scarves over our shoulders while the psalmist recited "for thou art with me". We later simulated "a table before me, in the presence of mine enemies" using the white satin which glimmered from the embedded glitter. In this moment, I felt my facial expressions changing. They mirrored the emotions associated with every word. We looked upward; scarves raised high behind us as "thou anointed my head with oil". The increased intensity of this moment connected me to God in a way that was nothing like the rehearsals. When we practiced, I was always trying to make sure I did everything right, yet on this day, a great sense of peace fell upon me. It was as though the spirit of the Lord swooped into the sanctuary for a one-on-one encounter with me. I closed my eyes even though I needed to watch and remain in sync with the rest of the ladies. The very moment the psalmist said, "He restoreth my soul", tears flowed from my eyes like a river. I could no longer fight it. There was no stopping this move of God. As my arms began to tremble, I used what little bit of control I had left to resist vocally crying out! I often wonder what would have happened if I just allowed myself to be free in that moment. Instead, I resisted, and because of this, it became a full-on struggle, inside and out. There had to be at least another minute or so left for the song, which for a dance can seem like forever. I thought, surely, I won't make it to the end without just throwing myself to the floor.

"...And I will dwell in the house of the Lord, forever!" (Psalm 23:6)

The song concluded with repetition of verse 6. Hearing over and over that I would "dwell in the house of the Lord forever" allowed it to fully settle in my spirit just how good God is and had been to me. I had other moments of confirmation, like my point of accepting Christ in 1990, and rededicating my life to Him in early 2003, but nothing compared to the peace and comfort that I felt while experiencing the presence of God so openly. I realized what it meant for the holy spirit to be in the place. The song concluded with repetition of the word "forever." We ended with great emphasis demonstrating grace (like in our name), waving our scarves, executing multiple turns, and concluding with a slow curtsy. Between tears, trembling arms, and nervousness about crying out loud, I welcomed the closing because it was more than I could bear. I needed to get where I felt it was okay to scream! We exited the sanctuary to the applause of the congregation, and I lost it. Just outside the door, I fell to the floor, screamed, cried, and thanked God for his presence in my life. I knew through that dance and the 23rd Psalm that I was restored. I honestly felt like a new person. I recognized God's presence and understood his protection in this moment, and I was free. God said it, and no matter how many others were in the sanctuary that day, I knew that was my special encounter with God.

Clarity

The coming months would be life changing as God's presence became more evident. His voice started becoming clearer. After the encounter from dance ministry, I experienced a desire to be in God's presence as much as possible. I became extremely restless thinking about all I wanted to do for the kingdom. All I wanted to do was learn. One of the greatest lessons on the journey was to be patient and wait on the Lord. I began reading, fasting, and praying more than ever. I started losing sleep because I would wake up, grab a book, and try to take in as much as I could. As I craved more time with him, I realized what God wanted me to do. My call to ministry was ultimately revealed. I became more mindful of my attitude and how I reacted in response to situations.

When I returned to school to study marriage and family counseling, some thoughts resurfaced about my hidden pain. I realized while working through a counseling course how I still carried the burden of losing my baby sisters. God used the academic setting to help me deal with various forms of grief. Because we alternated between the roles of counselor and client, I had an opportunity to work through those emotions. It was a Christian institution, so I gained a greater understanding of applying scriptures to my daily walk. Additionally, we prayed throughout the process, and again, I found peace. The feeling wasn't identical to the dance experience, but it provided what I needed in that season. As God continues to walk me through matters of the heart, I can let go of things I've somehow held on to. I know I will continue overcoming challenges as God uses me for His glory. He said I would, and I believe him with my whole heart.

2. DELAYED BUT NOT DENIED

Tamica R. Simon

As a very young child, I had no choice but to attend Sunday school, children's church, bible study, vacation bible school, Hallelujah night, you name it. I can even remember a time where I was not allowed to wear pants. I grew up in an era where children did not ask questions and most certainly not in the Bradford family. I was always an inquisitive child though and I will admit that it has gotten no better as an adult. I am a very logical and literal person, so of course I have struggled with God's existence despite my upbringing. I smile as I recall my grandmother saying, "you are so smart until you're stupid. You have all that book knowledge but no common sense". One thing is for sure though, and it is that each time my faith gets weak He shows me that He is the Great I AM!

Now, by no means am I an expert on God or religion and I probably never would have considered taking this project on, because in my eyes, I am no author! I am a runner and it can be on the streets, a track or from God. In nearing year's end though, I realized that I had ticked off nearly every item on my vision board except that closer walk that I claimed I wanted. A God encounter could be as simple as the realization that I can only make attempts to change my way of thinking by investing more time in my spiritual health. One way of doing that was by hiding myself away and getting in his word. I went back to daily bible plans. One month to the day that I was asked to be a part of this collaboration, I had completed a plan called "Seeing God" which was a reminder that he sees our hearts and knows what is done. If nothing else, this was confirmation of being on the right track and I should waste no more time running from God but rather to him.

My most recent encounters started as I was finishing up my degree. I was due to complete my MBA in December and was yet to find an internship. I have always had a heart for senior citizens and find myself relishing in their company at every visit to the VA Hospital. I can sit

2. DELAYED BUT NOT DENIED

for hours on end listening to stories from their early years. My dream is to one day open my own nursing home or adult day care center. In order to do this, I would need a license and have hit every possible roadblock in attaining my dreams. I'm quite tech savvy and love my microwave, cell phone and internet because they give instantaneous results. Anything less than that is a problem and doubt begins to set in. You begin to wonder if those dreams are in fact aligned with God's plan. I guess I needed to be reminded that my time was not his. Galatians 6:9 does tell us not to grow weary of doing good and that we will reap in due season as long as we don't give up. A month before graduation, I was told to contact a facility that I didn't even know existed despite having passed by there on countless occasions. Not only was the administrator happy to receive my call, but he wanted me to interview the very next morning.

I entered the doors of the building three weeks later and began greeting the staff and residents. I am one who never meets a stranger so of course I had to not only speak with those in the nursing home but in the assisted living and senior apartments as well. While exploring every nook and cranny of the facility, I stumbled upon the salon or beauty parlor as my grandmother called it. It was just like any typical salon, unless you count the chihuahua in the basket of someone's walker, and there was chatter about plans for the weekend. The ladies in the salon were getting their hair done for church on Sunday and invited me to come. See, we serve a jealous God. Despite me wanting a closer walk with him, I chose to work overtime at my regular job on Saturdays which required me to do four internship hours on Sundays. I scheduled myself to be at work by noon knowing very well the struggle of both making it to early morning service on time and the fact that I really did not like those services as much. Aside from the Holy Spirit, nothing quite convicts you like an elderly person reminding you of promises unkept, so I now needed to make their services too. Me and my big mouth!

Excuses eliminated, I had no choice but to make it to church when it was literally 2 doors down, and an elevator ride up from my office. There is no way to say I got lost. Needless to say, I was ill-prepared for these services. First of all, it was a full chapel, usher greeting you at the door, praise and worship, an anointed message and smiling faces all around. Even more so, I was not prepared for the knowledge that they had prayed for me a week prior. They had prayed for an administrator with a heart for his children. In the Pastor's more than 10 years at that

2. DELAYED BUT NOT DENIED

church, an administrator had never walked through those doors. The Pastor's wife had been an employee up until a couple of weeks prior, so they knew that God needed to send someone. Can you imagine wondering if you made the right decision and then receiving confirmation like this? Little did they know that I needed them just as much as they needed me.

Luke 12:48 says, "to whom much is given, much will be required". God had given me a unique opportunity to bless his people with my knowledge, talents and time. In that first week alone, I had many encounters with God and his people. I had a woman with dementia, who rarely spoke, grab my hands and pray for me like none other right in front of the nurse's station. It shook me to the core and I had to step away and get myself together. There is yet another who called me into her room to pray with her because she had missed church services and I looked like I knew the power of prayer. She turned out to be a member of my childhood church home and I will admit that I selfishly wanted her to stay. We had many such days of my being stolen off into her room to pray and I thank God for touching the hearts of those CNAs that caught us.

Too often we think that miracles are a thing of the past and something limited to biblical times. These are events placing all of the focus on God and challenging anyone to deny what happened. When you know better; you do better. Sometimes we have to recognize God's intervention in the normal workings of a situation. God was equipping me for service. Can you recall seeing friends laughing about an evening out and it seems you never got the invite? Do you remember having to console your child because his classmate could only have 6 children at his birthday, and he didn't make the cut? Well since we all know that pain too well, I refused to let people be excluded in what is now their home. If there is a holiday celebration, the God I serve said to just invite everyone, even their families back at home, and let them decide whether or not to come. Some responded by saying, "Oh my Mom won't attend, she's such and such religion" but there is just something about an infectious smile combined with the power of prayer. Those very residents were the first to roll themselves right on into that activity room and the smiles on all our faces said that I had found and answered my calling.

My grandparents were devout Christians. My parents were the same. We couldn't play cards or listen to secular music. There are certain things that were expected of me growing up just because of my last name. I am not my parents and those were some big shoes to fill. Honestly, wearing those shoes seems pretty uncomfortable even now. God wired me differently and I am O.K. with that. I can remember Mommy visiting my grandmother in the nursing home and them sitting in silence for hours on end. She would leave nearly in tears. I would go and we would talk up a storm. I had to call Mommy just to prove it. This was but one of the many times when I realized that I only needed to be me as my ministry is unique. The gift of gab is truly a gift. I have finally found a way to serve that matches my gifts. All this time I had been trying to find my niche in the world post-military and it also led me to my place within the church body.

God has given me a great deal but even more so he has entrusted the care of his children to me during their final days on this earth. Those seniors, who I was supposed to be helping, were the ones to remind me of my commitment to be a faithful steward. In a nursing home, you are always identifying obstacles and moving them out of the way. A slip hazard at that age can be the difference between life and death. It's like a light went off in my head and I immediately knew that I needed to do the same thing in my life. I needed a clear and clutter free path for God to continue to reach me. This also let me know just how perfect God's timing is. I'm sure it's only me, but my dining room table is huge and there is always space for one more book, magazine, piece of mail, cup, crafting project, etc. I know I should clear it off before moving on to something else, but because of its size and the fact that it's only me, I can just shuffle things around and utilize even more of the space. This sounds a lot like my life. I pile on family, and work, and school, and friends, and meetings, and organizations, and travel, and whatever else I am unable to say NO to. It is a lot of good intentions but a mess of clutter. One way or the other, God swept some of this out of my life and cleaned off the table immediately before giving me more.

You see, I started this journey upset and frustrated about not finding an internship. I was later reminded that Genesis 50:20 says, "you intended to harm me, but God intended it for good to accomplish what is now being done". At the end of the day, obstacles show your weaknesses and bring you to your knees so that you are in a position to see who is truly in control! It is at that point when you can truly see God. The Israelites wandered in the desert for 40 years before they could enter the Promised Land. Stress, anxiety and uncertainty will have you going in circles rather than stepping out of the

2. DELAYED BUT NOT DENIED

comfort zone and just going directly from point A to point B. God did not keep me in the wilderness forever, but He was sure to show me that my obstinance and disobedience caused my desires to be delayed if not denied!

Father God, I thank you for each and every encounter. I thank you that I can be my own person yet still continue to serve you. I ask that you allow me to continue to decrease so that you may increase. I want to use my gifts in a way that fulfills me as I glorify you; not for position or title but so that I may bless your children. You have come that we might have life and it is a promise of an abundant one. I thank you for meeting me where I am and the knowledge that you will never leave or forsake me. Amen.

3. DON'T RUN! WALK!

VERNETTA DUNBAR

One of my favorite bible stories is Jonah and the Big fish; some also call it, "Jonah and the Whale". This is one of many stories that has been taught to me as a small child in Sunday School and Vacation Bible School. The book of Jonah can be described as a parable. A parable is defined as a simple story used to illustrate a moral or spiritual lesson, as told by Jesus in the Gospels. The book of Jonah, with only four chapters, is unique in that there are several lessons that can be learned. Jonah's story contains strong warnings to all of God's people. It best personifies four different situations that we as humans often find ourselves in with our relationship with God. What do I mean? Let us look at each chapter.

In chapter one, we see Jonah **running from God.** How many times have you found yourself running from

God? God speaks to us in many ways. Sometimes when we hear from him, He is giving us instruction, but we tend to procrastinate or simply ignore Him (I've been there SEVERAL TIMES). God told Jonah to go to a city called Nineveh. Nineveh was a sinful and wicked city whom God loved and needed them to repent from their wicked ways. God needed Jonah to go to Nineveh to deliver a message of repentance. Jonah did not want to, so he ran away and hid. His hiding place was on a boat heading to a different city, Tarshish. Now one thing we should all know is that you cannot hide from God, the all-knowing God. While Jonah was on the boat, God sent rough winds and waves. The turbulence was so bad, Jonah was forced off the ship into the sea. Jonah was trying to run from God and found himself in the middle of the sea. As a result of being in the middle of a cold sea, Jonah became stuck. Have you ever been stuck in a situation with no place to go and no one to get you out? How many times were you in that place? What was your only option?

As we look at chapter two, Jonah had no choice but to **run to God**. God allowed a whale to swallow Jonah. He was stuck with no way out. He had hit rock bottom. He was scared, he feared his life was over. Jonah's only option was to pray (sounds familiar?). He prayed to God asking

3. DON'T RUN! WALK!

for forgiveness so that he can get out of the belly of this whale. I am so grateful to have a Big God! God's grace, love, and mercy has given us so many chances. He gave Jonah another chance by telling the whale to release him; and in chapter three Jonah is **walking with God.** Jonah obeyed the second time and went to Nineveh to deliver the message of repentance.

After receiving God's mercy and favor, Jonah started "feeling himself." He was not happy that God forgave the people of Nineveh. He felt that God should not have saved the city of Nineveh. He also felt that those people did not deserve to live. We all have experienced situations where God allowed things to happen to others that we felt were unfair. We become angry, jealous and cast judgement on others' situations and blessings. This leads us into chapter 4. Jonah expressed his anger and bitterness to God and as a result, God had to teach him another lesson (read chapter 4). We as humans have a right to feel the way we do, it's part of what makes us human; however, one thing that we should not do is judge another individual or God's decision to bless someone we feel doesn't deserve the blessing. This is another chapter, HA!

In summary, the book of Jonah points out four situations we find ourselves in the way we relate to our

God. We are either running away from God, running to God, walking with God, or running ahead of God. This chapter focuses on two of these situations that I feel are extremely critical in our Christian living, running to God and walking with God. These actions put us in position to have an Encounter like no other with God.

Running to God

There are two ways in which one can run to God. The first way; we are all familiar with is praying or talking to him. Prayer is a spiritual discipline. Spiritual Discipline puts us in front of God and puts us in position to hear from Him. The second way in which we run to God may not be familiar to some people; and that is God using situations to get our attention. When God asks us to do a task or call us to do certain things, sometimes we ignore him. Other times we may not hear Him. If you are like me, there were times that I heard Him speak but I became afraid or felt that I was not worthy enough. This can be thought of as running away from God. He will put us in situations where we have no choice but to run to him. Referring to Jonah, I truly believe that while in the belly of the whale, he was forced to think about his relationship with God and about what God called him to do. He prayed, he reaffirmed his faith in God and renewed his

3. DON'T RUN! WALK!

commitment to Him. He acknowledges that there is only one God, all others that appear to be in the likeness of God are just worthless idols. He vowed that he would keep his promise and pledged to sacrifice and acknowledge God's help. For it is the Lord who delivers people, not man.

God has a way of drawing people and arranging events so that people will turn to Him; for Jonah, it was placing him in the belly of a fish. Some people, the events may be financial issues, sickness, incarceration, or near-death experiences. Each one of us has a purpose or calling; we would not be here if we didn't. He calls each of us to do a specific task that benefits the Kingdom of God. This calling may be ministry in the church, teaching, being a foster parent, or a manager at a company. When we don't grasp that calling, or we hear the calling and choose to ignore it, God will give us no choice but to run to him. Sometimes, God will make you do some strange things, things you don't want to do, things, you may not like.

Fifteen years ago, God called me to be a minister. The last thing I wanted to do was to be a minister. My father was a pastor, I have seen his struggles and have witnessed some of the negative things that he and my mother experienced. Being a preacher's kid was not a glorious life at times; so, in my head, I knew for sure this was not something that I wanted to be a part of as an adult. I soon realized that this wasn't a decision for me to make. It became a simple answer of yes or no. Like Jonah, I tried to run away by procrastinating and making excuses because I did not feel that I had the personality, skills and patience to minister to a world of hurting people. It was not until one day when I was driving home from work that the Lord put me in that place.

The Encounter

On a normal workday driving home in 2005, I was driving down 476 S, also known to Philadelphians as the Blue Route, listening to the gospel station Praise 103.9; driving at a speed around 70 miles per hour when a song comes on titled, YES, by Shekinah Glory. Through the words of this song, the Lord spoke to me. Now, this was no ordinary encounter. The Spirit of the Lord literally surrounded me, my shoulders were weighed down, **HEAVY**! I could not move, still driving 70 miles per hour, all I heard were these words:

"Will your heart and soul say yes

Will your Spirit still say yes?

There is more that I require of thee

3. DON'T RUN! WALK!

Will your heart and soul say yes?

Open your heart and tell the Lord yes

Say I'll obey Jesus, I won't stray Jesus

I'll do what you want me to do

I'll say what you want me to say

I'll go if you lead me

I won't be afraid

I'll step out on your Word and declare glory

Submit your way to His, tell him yes, tell the Lord yes

He's saying there is more that I require of thee

So, let your heart and soul say Yes"

Tears started to flow, and they still are as I am writing this. This was an encounter that was indescribable. When I came out of that experience, I was parked in front of my house, I did not remember getting there. Can you imagine? The Lord was calling me, giving me another chance to answer his call to be a minister. I surrendered.

Why does God want us to have another chance? He gives us a second chance, sometimes a third and fourth chance (He is just so merciful!) because He loves us! He whispers, He speaks, He echoes because he wants to be in sync with us. When God says that He loves us, it's more than an emotion. It is an invitation for transformation. God's desire for transformation is one of the reasons that He puts us in that place to focus on Him. He wants us to experience His love, His grace, His mercy, and His compassion, so that we can share that experience with other people. As I think back over my life, He's been calling me since I was very young. It was my will so to speak not to listen, simply ignore Him because it's not what I wanted. BUT GOD! I am so grateful for that Encounter!

Walking with God

After telling God "Yes", I went through a period of preparation and discernment. In 2009, I had the privilege to attend the National Youth Worker's Convention in Atlanta. At the time I was serving as Director of Youth Ministries at a church in Lansdale, PA. My first night there, I heard a sermon that put the exclamation point on my period of discernment. It was just one verse that made clear to me why God called me to minister to others on

3. DON'T RUN! WALK!

His behalf. The scripture comes from the book of Revelation chapter 3 verse 11. It reads, "hold onto what you have, so that no one will take your crown." The biblical definition of crown is a symbol of your eternal rewards. My interpretation is that the crown can also be the calling God has upon your life for others to see. If you don't wear your crown, or accept and work in your God-given purpose, God will give it to someone else to fulfill. Ever experience something that was taken away from you and given to some else? A toy? A position? Now some of you may ask, If God is so merciful and compassionate, why would he take away my crown? In another biblical story, the "Parable of the Talents" (Matthew chapter 25); Jesus describes the story of three servants who are given various amounts of talents (a unit of currency) to invest. One servant is given five talents, another is given two talents to invest. They both invest their talents and double their money. The third servant was given only one talent. Instead of investing it, he hides it. The Master took his talent away from him and gave it to the one who had 10 talents.

God gives you a crown because He wants to be glorified in and through you. He wants to use you to bring others to Him. When you decide to wear your crown, you are telling God that you choose to submit to Him and walk with Him. When you walk with God, you become one with Him. There is a special glow that we receive that may not be apparent to us but it is apparent to other people, especially, non-believers.

God doesn't call those who are already equipped to do the job, He equips those He chooses to do the job. After my encounter, I went to my Pastor. I didn't know what to do or what it meant. Through my Pastor I was able to obtain the tools needed to effectively minister to others. I had to learn, even though some of my gifts came naturally, other duties of a minister required work and education. The series of steps that I needed to get to where I am and what I have accomplished so far did not come naturally. It required work and God orchestrated all of it. I needed more theological education, GOD sent me to Palmer Theological Seminary. I needed experience in leading people, He sent me to Christ United Methodist Church in Lansdale, PA and Aslan Youth Ministries in Red Bank, NJ. My attitude towards certain things and certain people needed adjustment so that I can be able to effectively minister to those who are hurting and in need of healing, God allowed many unfortunate situations to occur in my life. I didn't ask for anything…it just happened all because

3. DON'T RUN! WALK!

I said Yes to God and told Him I would walk with Him. Today I am a workplace Pastor; as I call it, managing two departments. I am the founder of Sacred Heart Ministry; through which Digest This! Magazine was authored and published.

With all that has transpired in our world today, now is the time to start wearing your crown. This world is in a state of Spiritual Upheaval, with a pandemic and economic distresses; people are in pain, they are desperate, hurt, angry and lost. This type of pain doesn't affect a specific gender, race, economic status, or social status. Things will not change; this world will not change until all of us submit and walk with God by walking in our God given purpose. There is an urgency for everyone to operate in their God given purpose. Yes, you will be afraid sometimes, yes you will be exhausted sometimes, yes, your feelings will get hurt sometimes. There is a difference though, God will reward and favor you in ways you could not possibly imagine. He will give you what you need without you even thinking about it. I'm a living witness. I'm going to continue to wear my crown and I'm going to wear it well because at the end of my journey, I don't want to have anything else left to give because I want God to say that I used all of what He gave me to help make His Kingdom powerful.

Stop running, start walking and you will be amazed of all that God wants to give you. Wear your crown and wear it well!

4. WON'T HE DO IT

April Joy Bowden

"Angels Watching Over Me"

I was about seven when I had my first spiritual encounter. At that tender age, I had lost my mother to cancer, been separated from my siblings, experienced separation and divorce of my new parents and all the joys that come with being shuffled between two caregivers. Although I did not fully understand all that was going on, I knew that this was not the type of life people my age was accustomed to living.

I was living in my eighth "home" with my old male caregiver and his new girlfriend and her two daughters (respectfully dad and mom). I adjusted to my new life….kinda. I recall bedtime being my "safe place". I did not have to talk to anyone, no one was asking if I was ok and the thoughts that raced through my mind during the day were quiet. That is, until I started having a recurring dream.

In the dream, I was a front seat passenger (before laws requiring children to sit in the back). It was just me and the driver. I don't recall ever seeing the driver's face. In the dream, we were crossing a bridge and the driver pushed me out of the car. I remember falling and crying on the way down. Every morning, I woke up disturbed by the dream. The dream felt like I had been allowed to watch a movie that wasn't age appropriate and I played the leading role. For a long time, the dream scared me. Every time I had the dream, it was the same bridge, the same fall, the same cries and the same feeling when I woke up. I wondered how I kept living in the dream. Surely, people who are pushed from such a height did not survive. One night, my dream was different. I realized how I lived through the fall. This time, I saw someone near the bottom that caught me. The next morning, remembering that I had been saved, I woke up relieved. I was confused, but happy to have a slightly different ending in the dream.

The occurrence of the dream lessened, but it did not go away. Around this time, an aunt who lived close by suggested my stepsisters and I start attending Sunday school and church with her and my cousin. I do not know what happened to church, but we were regulars at Sunday school. After attending Sunday school for a while, the dream began again. Each time, the dream had more clarity. The first thing I remember being different was that the "person" who caught me appeared to be floating. Eventually, I saw water in the dream. I was close to hitting the water when I was caught. Every time I woke up after being "saved", I felt better about the dream. I stopped concerning myself with who pushed me. I turned my thoughts to who saved me. I kept hoping to see a familiar face. Instead, I saw something that I remembered seeing in Sunday school, an angel. With all that I had been learning each Sunday, I was thrilled that it was an angel who came to rescue me.

As my spiritual walk blossomed and my level of interpretation grew, I decided that this was God's way to communicate to me than in life, people would push me and at times I would fall. But I could be assured that "He will command his angels concerning you to guard you in all ways; they will lift you up in their hands, so that you will not strike your foot against a stone." (Psalm 91:11-12)

"Love is Patient"

I have had some great and some not so great dating experiences. One relationship will always stick out to me. Most people have heard themselves say, "It couldn't be me." When we hear about troubles other people have in their relationships (infidelity, abuse, bad habits, etc.). I was that person until I found myself head over heels in love with a crack addict. By the time I processed fully what I was dealing with, I was in way too deep. During this period, I did some crazy things and went places I had no business. With both of our foolishness, I was always grateful that my prayers for our safety were always answered.

They said, "God protects babies and fools" and I was no baby. We dated for years and I continued my faith walk. On occasion, I invited J to church with me. My invitation was always declined, until that one time, it wasn't. I was planning to attend Watch Night Service and after all the times I was told no, I almost did not extend the invitation. We entered the building and found one of the few empty seats. Pastor preached a word that night. Near the end of the service, he instructed us to pray with expectation about what we wanted God to do for us in the coming year. I knew exactly what I would pray for and

4. WON'T HE DO IT

this year, it was not myself. With a heavy heart that was breaking and tears in my eyes, I prayed for J's deliverance from drug addiction. I prayed that prayer every night. I prayed when J was at work. I prayed when J was asleep safely in our apartment. And I triple prayed when J was in the streets (sometimes for days).

Months went by and I told myself that there were a lot of prayers that went up that night and perhaps, He just had not gotten to mine. I was getting weary. Although I am a daily prayer warrior I had never sent the same prayer up so many times with no answer. I remember going to church one Sunday in May and the preacher talked about unanswered prayers (particularly prayers from Watch Night). He instructed those of us who still had not received an answer to keep praying. He assured us that the answer and the blessing was coming. I won't lie, I was frustrated. But the instruction put some fuel back in my hope and my patience. I decided I would put a little extra in and decided to fast. I got through the first day and thought how quickly the next thirty-nine days would go. I was so wrong. The next six days were tough and during my fasting and praying (still for addiction deliverance), J had a binge and was gone for days. I felt defeated. But I remained vigilant. At the end of my forty days, I felt renewed that my prayer would be answered soon.

The universe felt like it was shifting until the next weeklong disappearance. I remained steadfast and I started preparing myself for His will and what I was certain would be the end of our relationship. I am not sure we ever officially broke up, but I was done. I changed the locks at the house and threw my hands up. Things could have gone sideways. But, on July 31st I took my beloved to a detox center (J's request). I went to visit when I could and on completion of the program, J went to live in a recovery house.

Every year we do a shoutout on social media. My post is usually a message of congratulations for staying clean and a message of strength, hope and encouragement. My most recent July 31st post read, your presence in my life has been one of my biggest challenges and one of my biggest rewards. They say things in life are either a lesson or a blessing. You've been both. Prayer changes things and I am grateful He heard and answered my prayers for your deliverance. Welcome to your teen years. #13yearsclean

4. WON'T HE DO IT

"Open Doors"

I remember hitting the floor and gasping near tears at the pain I felt trying to get up. A trip to the doctor confirmed what I thought. It was broken. My left ankle would require surgery. I had a bunch of questions for the doctor in urgent care. I jokingly asked if the break meant that the half marathon I had trained twelve weeks for and was supposed to run in six days was off the table. He chuckled and said he advised against participating.

I was able to be seen at the orthopedic quickly. I had even more questions. I wanted to know how soon we could have surgery scheduled and how long I would have to wear a cast. I had accepted a job that would start soon, and the job would require me to be out of the cast and an all clear to participate. The job was out of state, so I also needed to be done with follow-up appointments. He told me that he could do the surgery that week and that if I healed well, I would be able to get the cast off 48 hours before I needed to report. I knew I would be cutting it extremely close, but I was hopeful.

I asked if I could continue with my current job. He told me I would have to be non-weight bearing and that if my job could make accommodations, I could work. I asked about driving and he said I could drive once I was off the pain medications and felt comfortable.

In all my enthusiasm, I didn't think about all of the things I had taken for granted that I was able to do. The reality of it all hit pretty quickly.

My job required travel. Would I be able to drive long distances with a cast comfortably? Let me tell you how God works. I never had to find out if I would be comfortable. My schedule changed and all my work for six weeks was within a twenty-minute drive. It was rare for me to be home for more than ten days. Six weeks was more than a blessing.

I wondered how I would manage doing my hair if I had to keep my foot propped. A few weeks prior to breaking my ankle, I met a woman who braided hair. She happened to text me right after the surgery to check in. I couldn't have been happier to receive that timely check in. When I told her about my ankle, she asked if I would be comfortable with her coming over to do my hair. Not only did she braid my hair, she noticed I had dishes in the sink and she washed them. I had a trash can that was near full and she insisted on emptying it on the way out. God's timing was perfect in our meeting and her text.

4. WON'T HE DO IT

I was apprehensive about my ability to do the job I was so excited about that would be starting soon. How could I effectively lead a staff and residents at a location that stressed physical activity from a knee scooter. I wondered how I would conduct an open house with the same limitations at a fitness camp. Would the parents be comfortable leaving their children with a person who couldn't participate in the activities they would hope their children would do?

My new employer was very accommodating. They sent a staff member to help with open house. During our preparation and tour of the campus, I rode my knee scooter up to the baseball field with my assistant. After rolling around for a bit, I realized that I had ascended a decent size hill and there was no way I was going down on one leg and four wheels. He had to go get his car to take me back down. I skipped that part of the tour during the open house.

My team that year was amazing. The first few weeks, they adjusted to a leader who moved slowly and supported me as I transitioned from driving to meals (it was a long walk) to getting my crutches to walk with the crew to walking it on my own. The craziest thing about this job is that the position I worked was not the position I had applied for. I wanted to be an instructor so that I could do the physical activities with the campers to help them meet their fitness and weight loss goals. At the beginning of my interview, the interview presented me with the opportunity to fill a position that had not been listed. Had I gotten the job I applied for; I would have had to turn it down.

"When He opens doors, no one can shut." Isaiah 22:22

As each camper arrived at the start of each session, I had them write down a goal to accomplish before the end of camp, including a time to complete their mile in. I had the team do the same. My goal was to walk to the baseball field unassisted (I had to drive most of camp) and complete a mile. The night before camp ended for the summer, my campers that started with me in week one walked the hill to the baseball field with me and cheered me on as I completed my mile.

One of my big concerns while I was in my cast and boot and using crutches was how I would juggle the crutches and my things and open doors.

4. WON'T HE DO IT

Even when I approached a door and there was no one there, every time I got near the handle, someone always appeared to open it. I was more than grateful for God's perfect timing.

5. HEAR HIS VOICE AND OBEY

DEBLEN B. EDGE

Why am I up at 5:30 a.m. on a Saturday? I am so glad you asked. Well, I am going through a gamut of feelings and excitement. I feel so honored to have been invited to participate in this book project, which comes on the heels of my poetry book project which is about to be released. Dealing with the illness and eventual death of my mother just about eight months ago, I learned that I have a rare bone marrow disorder (cancer). So, to decide which way to go, I thought going a bit further back would be better. Recent situations are so fresh, and I would be crying all the time that I would not be able to finish this project. I am going to start about six years ago, but never fear I have had encounters with God all my life.

He goes with me everywhere I go and is waiting for me when I get to my destination.

After retiring from the military in 1999 and working as a federal contractor for a while, in 2010 I was finally able to start my first federal government job. This is just a little background leading to what I think was one of the most important eye-opening moments for me about how God works. In January of 2010 excited about my new job and ready to work, little did I know one small incident would later force me to stay or go and that decision would eventually lead to a life-altering incident in 2014. It happens that my supervisor at my brand new good government job was very difficult to work for and it was the sentiments of all my co-workers, but long story short, I was given a project to do and each time I presented her the results, she was insistent that my results were not what she asked for. Point to remember – she would change the requirement after she had given me the project but never gave me the change – so amid the back and forth and showing her my extensive notes about each of her requests, she still insisted that it was not what she wanted, upon which I responded to her, "I can't read your mind when you change it from your original request." This happened on Friday. Well, to my surprise when I showed up for

5. HEAR HIS VOICE AND OBEY

work Monday morning, I was called to the conference room, where my supervisor, her supervisor, and the Department head all waited for my arrival. At that time, she presented me with a termination letter. Now, I am floored, not believing that these people were letting her serve this letter. She already had two equal employment opportunity (EEO) complaints against her, and because of our conversation a few days prior she thought I had filed the same kind of report. I went to request a mediator to conduct a meeting with my supervisor to see if we could resolve our issues. Once I went to my union representative after being served the termination letter, they met with management. I was offered a letter to state that her termination letter had been rescinded and I had two choices. I could stay and continue to work for this supervisor, or I could resign with no adverse actions. I was told that these options were offered this way because of my job specialty. There was no other place in the organization they could reassign me.

Some years later while working another federal government job it was time to renew my clearance. I worked in personnel security and I knew that honesty and truthful information were required. I could not leave anything to be questioned. I explained the situation to the investigator and awaited the process which took approximately two years. In February 2014, I received a package with attachments explaining that my clearances were being revoked. Now not only am I floored; I am crushed. Going through the package I discovered that the investigator reported that I had resigned from a job after being told I was fired. Of course, this was not the case, nor what I explained to the investigator. My explanation included that for the lack of supporting documentation and concrete foundation for the termination letter, management rescinded the termination letter. In my rebuttal back to the adjudicator for my case, my rebuttal was denied, and they stuck with their finding that I had lied on my clearance renewal form. I was offered an opportunity to go to court with witnesses and character letters. I contacted the previous office I worked in, specifically the young lady I trained for my former job. The Deputy Director did not have time or acted as if they didn't know what to say, nor would they agree to write character letters. That came as a shock. Even without their support I was able to get what I needed and proceeded to go to court armed with three witnesses and many character letters.

5. HEAR HIS VOICE AND OBEY

My current supervisor and branch chief at the time were aware of all these actions, so they offered to help this matter, insisting even if the rulings were to take my clearances they would assist me in finding a job within the unit that did not require a clearance until such time I could get mine renewed. When the final decision came, the rebuttal court stayed par for the course and revoked my clearances. My supervisor and branch chief suddenly developed selective amnesia, not remembering the promise of their support. With the court decision and that decision of my supervisor and branch chief, I was then served with a termination letter effective July 25, 2014. What could I say? My life was falling apart one piece at a time and going into a rapid tailspin, not to mention how I felt knowing how I would be affected financially. I would go from making a pretty good salary down to a little less than one-third of that in a matter of months. Yes, I had savings and my 401K, but that would not last forever. As hard as I tried, I could not get a job anywhere, in the meantime funds were getting shorter and shorter. In an attempt to make it a little easier I contacted my mortgage company to get a modification and was promptly told they could not do one because I was not behind in payments. When times did get to where I could not pay the mortgage payments, I contacted my mortgage company again and this time I was then told I did not make enough money to get a modification; then foreclosure and short sale packages began to come. In the meantime, while my mother's health was beginning to fail, I was having health problems of my own. I was still in shock from the activities of the past few months. Did I mention all this was happening about two or three months before my 60th birthday? By this time, I was heartbroken, feeling defeated and scared because I had been on my own so long, making my way while fixing problems without a second thought.

Let me digress a minute. This is not the first time I have been without a job, but when I was, a new job always came almost immediately, never more than a month. Often I would leave a job on Friday and start a new one on Monday. I always credited these easy transitions to God smiling on me. Notice, I gave God the credit. I was doing so well at one point earning a six figure salary, for which I gave God the credit. Curled up in my trusty recliner one night not knowing what was going to happen next, trying to pull ideas out of my head, crying harder with each thought, with no one to call and a big decision to make, I cried myself to sleep. It seems subconsciously overnight a decision came to mind. Depressed and

5. HEAR HIS VOICE AND OBEY

heartbroken, I was feeling like a failure. I felt I'd also failed God. In my mind, God gave me this house and he decided to take it back, so I promptly started to gather boxes and other packing materials. I made plans of which room to start with.

One day as I was going through and sorting things, God planted a thought for me to call the Social Security Office. I ignored it for a few days because I connected social security with getting old, and I just knew I was not that old "(…and it's okay to laugh right here")". A couple of days later I received another one of those packages from my mortgage company, so I called them in hopes of biding some more time. On that call I learned that the hold up for modification was $500, I needed to prove in some way I was making $500 more a month in income and the package could be pushed through for possible approval. Again, feeling defeated, I began to cry as I packed and prayed to let God know I understood that what He gives He can take away. Low and behold again to the front of my mind popped Social Security. By this time my thoughts were, "ok Lord I hear you." I called the Social Security Office, explained my situation, and asked for a letter showing how much I would get when I started to receive benefits. I am going to take a leap here and say this phone call was not only very informative but was a slow beginning to the breakthrough journey God was about to send me.

On this call, a pleasant customer service agent listened to my story. After a brief question and answer period, he explained I could have been getting my husband's benefits since I turned 60 years old. Here I am a few months before turning 62, now, talk about being floored. Seems like I stayed on the floor during this time in life. But I had to stay focused because the operative words in that statement were "could have". Continuing, I was informed I could receive his social security until my own started, which was the amount I needed. Small steps towards tackling my situation. I gave in and registered to start receiving my Social Security benefits because I was informed that I would receive more from my benefits than from that of my husband.

Upon receiving the necessary letter, I sent it to the mortgage company, and after several conversations, they gave signs of possibly changing their minds. I found myself praising God every time I mailed something back and talked on the phone until the modification was finally done. Now being able to breathe a little and even though things were still going to be a struggle, praising God for

5. HEAR HIS VOICE AND OBEY

His blessings was ALL I could do. Right about the beginning of 2017 and making ends meet by the sweat of my brow things were getting more difficult because I had depleted my savings and 401K. But, here comes God again. I met someone whose passion was helping Veterans get their well-deserved benefits. I was advised of several things to do. Of course, I didn't do it right away, but by November of that year not being able to take it any longer and seeing myself headed back in the direction I had just come from, I was more than ready to complete the list of actions I had to submit to the Veterans Administration (VA). The package was complete and submitted with little hope for any action, but the wish for anything, the waiting game began.

Let me stop here for a short commercial of just how good God is: most people around me know about my infamous New Year's Day celebration at my home with gifts under the tree for all who attended. It started as a small function in 1997 for a few friends of mine that were so busy during Thanksgiving and Christmas times taking care of their families and elderly parents, that after the holidays they would complain they needed a break. My gift to them was an invitation to my house for brunch that I would cook. They could leave families and others they took care of at home for a few hours to just relax. Everyone needs a moment to not have to care about anyone but themselves at least one day of the year. This function became a big hit. So much so that one year a young lady asked if she could bring her husband. From then till now I have hosted this huge function every year. I said that to say this: not once, no matter how difficult my situation seemed to be going, God always made a way for me to continue the New Year's function. There were several years I was going to cancel because I could not figure where the money would come from without asking for help, but God always made a way for me to fund the whole function without canceling or asking for help. That's how God makes a way out of no way.

Okay back on track, sometime near the beginning of April 2018 needing to pay an unexpected bill I checked my account and nearly passed out. I noticed way more money than I was supposed to have. When I say way more, I mean *waaay* more. The first reaction was to call my bank to let them know they made a mistake. I called and the bank said no, not a mistake. Looking back at my account in case they were again mistaken, to my surprise I saw there was a deposit from the VA. My obedience to hearing the Lord in my ear, filing my claim with the VA;

5. HEAR HIS VOICE AND OBEY

I got my rating increased to 100%. This gave me the confirmation I was going to stay in the home that God gave me, everything was going to be alright and my worries were no longer an issue. That is a great feeling knowing God is always on the throne of grace and mercy. I have had many encounters with God, but this one I believe impacted my life to the core as well as forced me to examine and correct some things I thought were fine in my Christian life. The lesson learned for me from this encounter is no matter what is going on, always, keep strong faith and never take my eyes off my Lord and Savior Jesus Christ.

6. MY STORY; MY TESTIMONY

Rev. Marva J. Cumberbatch Wilson

This is My Story! My Testimony!

Thirteen years ago I traveled to Hemet California to visit my daughter and son-in-law with excitement, intending to help as they prepared for the birth of our second grandchild. The initial plan was for my husband and I to travel together, arriving before the due date. Unfortunately, due to his work schedule I ended up traveling alone with plans for him to join us later. By the grace of God I arrived that Friday evening to sunny California. After settling in, plans were made for me to sleep in and rest on Saturday, go to church with them on Sunday morning, return to their home, eat dinner, and relax until my daughter's scheduled doctor appointments on Monday.

My First Encounter

Immediately after church service Sunday morning, I went to the restroom and stood in line for what seemed like an eternity. Finally, it was my turn and as soon as I entered and closed the door behind me, I felt this intense pain in the back of my neck straight to the top of my forehead. The pain was more intense than anything I had ever experienced before. What I was experiencing was worse than a migraine or tension headache. I knew I was in trouble, so I immediately began to pray and to call on the name of Jesus. My plea was for him to help me feel well enough to make it out of the restroom to rejoin my daughter and son-in-law in the lobby. I remember the pain being so debilitating that I couldn't muster the strength to call out to anyone in the flesh, but in the spirit, I called the name of the Lord for help while clinging to the bathroom door for life. The more I prayed, the more I noticed that the pain began to fade. I continued to pray in my spirit: God I need your help. Please help me to get out of this restroom safely. I became aware that there was no one else in the restroom. Then I realized I was all alone, but never alone.

6. MY STORY; MY TESTIMONY

The Lord heard my plea and led me out of that restroom after what seemed like an eternity. If it were not for the Lord, I would have been passed out on that restroom floor because my energy was depleted. Thank You Lord for your saving grace! Thank You for taking me directly back to my daughter and son-in-law. On our forty-five minute drive back to their home, I laid in the back seat and shared my experience with them. Then the pain returned with a vengeance. The air and visibility were poor due to the California wildfires. There was gray snowflake like particles flying all over the place. I just wanted to go home and lay down. Upon our arrival to their home, I had something to eat, took two ibuprofens, and went to bed. I prayed and cried out to the Lord, until I fell asleep.

It was now Monday morning, and I was grateful the pain had eased. My son-in-law left to go to work, and my daughter and I went to her doctor appointments. They did her ultrasound and we were able to see my grandson and hear his heartbeat. After an early lunch, we went to her second and last appointment. While she was in the examination room, I went to the restroom and the pain returned with such intensity that I was barely able to move. Again, I cried out to the Lord for help and by his grace and mercy I was able to open the door and ask for help. My daughter and her doctor came, and I found myself in the emergency room once again. Hours later, I was finally seen by the Emergency Room doctor who said that my blood pressure was more than 250/100. I was given a prescription and was released. The next day things worsened, sending me back to the emergency room for a second time. Hours later, of enduring chronic pain, and unable to retain food, water or medicine, I was finally seen without resolve; just another prescription, and ice packs for my neck and forehead. At this point I knew that it was time for me to return home to my husband in North Carolina.

Tuesday morning, per my request my daughter and son-in-law took me on the forty-five minute ride to the airport. Unfortunately, airline staff would not allow me to fly. They were afraid I would take a turn for the worse which would force them to make an emergency landing. My daughter and her husband were paged, and they drove me back to their home. It was out of my control, they ended up taking care of me. My husband would be on the next available flight to California.

6. MY STORY; MY TESTIMONY

My Second Encounter

That night I got so sick I felt like I was dying. Whatever energy or breath I had left was slipping away. I was constantly crying out to God for help! Lord have mercy on me. Constantly repeating the Twenty Third Psalm and reminding Him of his promises. Lord you said, "You'll never leave me nor forsake me." (Hebrews 13:5 KJV) I was crying out to God, while fighting to survive. I was so weak, I needed reinforcement. I asked the Lord who He would have me to call and he brought to mind my spiritual mothers: Minister Sams and Rev. Allen, both in North Carolina where it was already past midnight. I called Minister Sams who we lovingly called Sister Sams. She promptly answered her phone as if she were awaiting my call. She could tell in my voice something was wrong and immediately told me not to say another word. I was on my knees while she began to pray, crying out to God and interceding on my behalf. I could feel the atmosphere shifting and the presence of the Holy Spirit. She told me to get some rest and I felt peace; like I had entered God's rest. My next memory was being in the bathroom throwing up profusely and feeling like everything inside of me was being pushed out of my body. I prayed my way back to my room and went to bed. I felt like I had entered into God's presence, He held me in His arms and cradled me. I was blessed to experience the most peaceful sleep I ever had in my entire life, and I didn't want to leave.

Wednesday morning, the pain returned with a vengeance. I could not believe what was happening. My life was slipping away, and I knew I didn't want to go to hell. I pleaded in my spirit " Lord please don't let me die." I had not made any preparations, and I wanted the opportunity to take care of some unfinished business. I needed to live in order to get right with God. Also, I needed to talk to family and others to redress any grudges, or resentments I was holding against them. Because I had experienced such peace in God's presence, I knew I needed to be with Him as my final destination. I was reminded that we are just sojourners upon this earth, and we need to live for Him.

My Third Encounter

After many prayers, multiple emergency room visits, a CAT Scan, a spinal tap, and being pumped with narcotics, I was still in serious trouble. My husband made it to our daughter's home and drove me forty-five minutes from Hemet to Loma Linda Hospital in Loma Linda, California. The emergency room was crowded, with no

6. MY STORY; MY TESTIMONY

available seats. Imagine having to wait ten hours in the backseat of a hot rental car in excruciating pain, praying the twenty-third Psalm in my spirit, while drifting in and out of sleep. The pains were coming and going like contractions, but more severely than what I had experienced when I gave birth to each of my three lovely children. I was exhausted after having no water, no food and no medicine. I was out of it. But God! Only God could have gotten me through this process.

Some of my recollections of being admitted are vague, and my husband had to fill in the blanks. I remember finally being able to lay on a bed, seeing the bright light in the room, and hearing voices around me. Thank God for blessing me with the ability to pray, endure, and persevere. I was admitted to the hospital. They took me upstairs to the ward and placed me in a room. There was a lot of commotion in the room and they injected something into my IV. It ran through my veins and I let out a horror movie scream. Doctors and nurses were all over me doing what they were trained to do. I vaguely remember a nurse taking my hand assuring me they were taking good care of me and everything was going to be alright. She informed me she was scheduled off for a few days, but she and other prayer warriors were praying for me and I was going to be okay. Yes! That nurse was one of God's ministering angels.

It was now Thursday, my daughter's due date. My grandson would be welcomed into the world at any time. Instead of helping her, I was sedated in a hospital bed, connected to a catheter, with no answers. That evening my husband returned and told me he had good and bad news. He handed me a Polaroid picture of my grandson and I cried tears of joy as he shared that the delivery went well, but my grandson was in a helicopter in route there to the Neonatal care ward because they identified a problem with his heart. It was surreal! My daughter gave birth to her baby boy who was being medically evacuated to the same hospital as his grandma. My husband went down to meet our son-in-law and I began to pray: " Lord, have mercy on us; my daughter needs you, my grandson needs you, I need you. Lord, we all need you! Please help us through these perilous times. We can't do it without you. Right this second, this minute, we are calling on you to work a miracle. We need your healing touch! You know all about our troubles. Deliver us from this evil. Lord your word said "we have not because we asked not" (James 4:2 KJV), but here I am Lord petitioning and interceding on behalf of my daughter and grandson. Touch them from the crown

6. MY STORY; MY TESTIMONY

of their heads to the soul of their feet. Touch every tissue, every bone, every marrow, every organ in their body. Fix it Lord like you said you would. I'm declaring (Isaiah 53:5 KJV) " By your stripes we are all healed." It is with thanksgiving that I pray, giving you all the praise, all the glory and all the honor. In your son Christ Jesus name. Let it be so Lord! Please let it be so! Amen."

" But rise and stand upon thy feet for I have appeared unto thee for this purpose, to make thee a minister and a witness both of these things which thou hast seen, and of those things in the which I appear unto you." (Acts 26:16, KJV).

Through the test!

Looking back, our faith was tested in more ways than one, but with God's help, we made it through. My daughter was discharged from the hospital in Hemet. She came to Loma Linda and wheeled me down to see my grandson. We were in the neonatal waiting room when the Lord gave us an assignment. He shifted our focus to other families who were in the need of prayer. There was a young couple whose baby needed emergency surgery due to a big growth on the neck that was cutting off circulation. There was a young woman who ran into complications due to preeclampsia. There was a mother with her daughter who recently gave birth and was sitting directly across the room in anguish because her premature baby was in ICU. While waiting to see my Grandson, we spoke to these families and prayed for and with them. The Holy Spirit was present as we prayed for their individual needs. It was never about us and always about Him! Those tests were and always will be about Him. He was preparing us for ministry, and it took preparation to get there. "After the test, the testimony." Our test began with our dependency on God and experiencing Him throughout the process. Both my grandson and I spent seven days in the same hospital. When I was finally able to hold him in my arms, he cuddled up to my left shoulder, looked at me, and went straight to sleep. God will meet us wherever we are, and He is faithful to his word. "He promised never to leave us nor to forsake us, (Hebrews 13:5). "he will be with us always, even until the end of the world." (Matthew 28:20, KJV).

Almost fourteen years later, I am grateful to be able to share my testimony, "My encounters with God." God is always waiting for an opportunity to speak with us. We need to make ourselves readily available to Him to develop a more intimate and personal relationship with Him. He

6. MY STORY; MY TESTIMONY

should be our number one priority. Setting aside time to enter his presence through prayer or meditation, reading devotionals or our bibles, or giving Him praise and worship, all critical to our spiritual growth. We each have a testimony but for Him to get the glory we must share them with others. My encounters with God have been the most rewarding and fulfilling times of my life, and I know there will be more before it is all said and done.

7. BRIDGING GAPS: GOD'S GIFT TO ME

Donna "DeeDee" Suttles

My grandparents had 15 children, 11 boys, and 4 girls. My grandparents and my father were big on family traditions. "Get in here!! Stop running in and out of this house or you will stay in," my grandmom would say!! My grandmother and grandfather kept us all during the summer months, Christmas break, and sporadic times throughout the year. My siblings, my cousins, and I LOVED going there. Pop-pop did many jobs. Among those jobs, he was a farmer known to have the best vegetables that you could sink your teeth into. Tomatoes, squash, corn, cabbage, beans... my cousins and I would sit on the grass and eat fresh cucumbers and tomatoes…right out the garden, and then run to get fresh water from the well. My grandmother told us if we fought one another we had to go home. Needless to say, we didn't fight because nobody wanted to leave such a place.

My grandparents' home was like a country version of Disneyland. There were all sorts of things to do and ANIMALS to watch and ride. My uncle Jimmy and Uncle Sam would bring their horses to the stables but before putting them up for the night they always took us for a ride down the street and back up. It was so magical seeing these horses; they were huge but yet so beautiful. I loved to pet the horses, but sometimes it seemed the horses were looking at me. My aunt Bea said it was because of all the people in my spirit and that was a good thing. I didn't understand that until I got older. My grandmother was the absolute BEST! She would have us girls (about 6 at a time) in the kitchen helping with supper. There was always something for everyone to do. Mixing the corn muffins was my thing and then pouring them in the cast iron muffin pan. Anyway, my grandmother often went to church. I knew when she was all dolled up and put on these pearl earrings and a pearl necklace that she loved and sometimes a hat that she was on her way to church. She talked often about God and being a good person. She would say, God can see you when you think nobody else can see you and to pray.

7. BRIDGING GAPS: GOD'S GIFT TO ME

Discovering my gift

I am one of 8 siblings and my Dad was military. He did not tolerate foolishness and he taught us about love and being fair. We never had a problem with skin color. I so love that man. Because our family was so loving, I couldn't wait until summer to see my cousins, aunts, and uncles. We would have such a great time running around Pop-pop's house and running in and out the gardens and apple orchards which were directly across the street from my grandparent's house. At night we would play hide and go seek in the cornfields and all around the house just hiding anywhere that we could. It was then I was stopped dead in my tracks as I saw someone standing there. I said to the person "Hello, <Waving my hand> who are you?" The person did not speak; they just stood there. There was this strange, funny feeling in the pit of my stomach. I tried but I couldn't tell if it was a lady or a man because it was dark' but I could see the silhouette clearly if that makes sense. I said to my cousin Sondra, "Do you see them?" because they were standing in front of us, but Sondra ran past them as if no one was there. My cousin Stephanie eventually asked me to stop trying to scare them. They ran into the house on numerous occasions and told my grandmother what happened.

Finally, my grandmother told me to come into the house. She sat me down and asked why I was trying to scare everybody telling them people were there when they were not. "But Mom mom, they ARE there and I SEE them! I am not trying to scare them. I'm trying to make sure they don't knock them over when they are running to the home base!" My grandmother listened, then said, "After you take your bath, I want to talk to you."

Understanding my gift

Once we all stopped playing, and my grandmom tucked everybody into bed I had to go into her room and talk to her. I didn't understand what the big deal was but anytime my grandmother said anything to us we all would listen. My gift must've been revealed to her in some sort of way because she said to me, "Listen to what I am about to tell you. Those people that you see are there, but everybody else cannot see them like US; you cannot go around telling people that you see them because they will think you are touched in the mind." I later found out, touched in the mind means crazy or mentally unstable in some sort of way. She then told me that I have a special gift and God was going to use me one day. I didn't know what God using me one day meant but I liked the idea of God using me!! She went on to say, "Do not be afraid of

7. BRIDGING GAPS: GOD'S GIFT TO ME

your gift. I have it too! We can see and hear things that other people cannot. And God has a special place for you in the world, DeeDee." She said I would have to wait until I can understand it, and no matter WHAT, it is a gift and a blessing from God. She said, "Not everyone has what you have." From that day on, I never really let them know when I would see or know things.

One day my cousins and I went walking down the hill to Vaticks store (a little 5 and dime) and as always, we were in the middle of the street. In a panic, I started yelling "Get out the street! He said, GET OUT THE STREET!!!"(He being the voice I heard).

Everybody ran to the side, although puzzled they moved... and then they started yelling at me saying, "You play way too much; what are you doing?" They were pushing me and yelling, but then out of nowhere a truck came and went straight down the middle of the street! It was going from side to side obviously out of control like he was intoxicated or something. Looking puzzled, they asked how I knew that truck was coming. I said I didn't know it, it was just someone telling me to get out of the street; "So I told you guys to get out of the street!" Things like that just seemed to happen more times than not. My cousins began to love having me around! My cousin

Sondra even called me the good luck charm. But it wasn't me at all; it was God using me at a very young age. I just didn't know it, but I sure enjoyed the attention that came from my cousins. I learned to trust the voice—which I know is God!

I remember being at the funeral some years later when my grandmother passed away. I understood very well that when they closed that box lid (casket) people could not get out, so I was trying to figure out how my Grandmom would get out of that box if they closed it. I started freaking out! "How is she dead if I sometimes still hear her?" Although deceased she still told me things and assured me she was fine. I knew the color of her dress even before we saw her. I know it was her that told me the color and in my dreams, we still laughed together. I started screaming and telling her to talk so that they would not "lock her in." I created such a scene that one of my uncles/family friend picked me up and took me to the car kicking and screaming. I remember my aunt Bea praying over me a week later. Uncle Paul said, "God likes that when you pray, and don't forget to thank him." I began to have visions all the time, and by the time I was 15 things were just so clear. I believe my pain of love and loss was so

7. BRIDGING GAPS: GOD'S GIFT TO ME

that I could speak God's word from a point of self-pain and be humble to help someone else.

Using my gift

God truly wanted me to tell people certain things to give them comfort, hope, or peace. Most of the time I knew things were going to happen before they happened. Can you imagine prophesying as a teenager?!! But in those days it was considered strange. My grandmother's words never left my heart. The holy spirit allowed my gift to show me things. I knew when people had passed away before anyone told me, I knew about other people's joy and happiness even before they happened; things like job promotions, marriages, divorces, surgeries, pregnancies, and the sex of someone's baby...you name it. I just knew things before they happened.

The day I got engaged was interesting because God said "Say NO, because he's not going to be your husband" but I was young and wanted to wear the ring. I dated him for 4 years but always said no to marriage. One day I was with my friend at Loockerman Exchange, a Supper Club and across the room was this tall, dark and handsome guy. I saw him looking at me as I was looking at him as well. Thank God I was single! He came over, we exchanged numbers and began to talk on the phone for hours every day. I even sent him a long stem rose to his room. Ha! Daniel was military at the time. I KNEW this was my husband. God said --- YES-- he is your husband! I told my sisters and my aunt Mary (My running partner at the time) and Doris Henry (MY DAY ONE FRIEND). I will tell you about our friendship later. Anyway, after 6 months we would marry; 32 years later, still going strong! Hallelujah!! Moving on, A moment that would change my life, hearing the words your father had a massive heart attack, a blockage of 94%, standing in the hospital, pacing, and praying, I said: "God if you'll save my father I will do whatever you need me to do, whenever you tell me to do it!!" My Father is 82 now, Praise God!!

Matters of life and death

There was a pregnant lady on one of my jobs for whom God specifically gave me instructions. God told me to tell her that she would be prescribed a medication, but not to take it. I haven't always been obedient to give messages like this, but in this case, I told her. She laughed and said, "I think the doctors know what they are doing DeeDee." Weeks later she was given medication, but she said she researched it and it was on her list of meds that she should not take. While receiving thanks from her and

7. BRIDGING GAPS: GOD'S GIFT TO ME

her husband, she said the doctor's words were, "The medication would have made you have a spontaneous abortion." I thanked and praised God with her.

My husband reminded me of an encounter while we were in the Bahamas. There was a gentleman on the beach and there was a line of people waiting to speak to him. He was supposed to be very wise and could "see" things. When he got to us he told Daniel a lot of true things even though Daniel tried to trick him. When he got to me he said, "You don't need this, you can do what I do. You have visions already!" One of the craziest experiences after that was when I realized I could sense things through smells. I was in New York for an event with two of my closest friends and when we arrived at the Marriott it was a beautiful hotel but I made such a big fuss because to me my room smelled like smoke. It was so strong that I called the front desk and requested someone come up because obviously someone somewhere was smoking. The manager came up to check but he could not smell a thing. I then asked if he could go to the room on the side of me and see if they were smoking. He said "no problem" as we watched him walk over and knock on the door. He stepped in and then came back and said there was no smoking going on nor was there a scent. Lynette said she couldn't smell the smoke. Meanwhile, Lynette's dad had been trying to reach her, and she managed to talk to him once. Sadly, we would later find out Lynette's dad died on the cruise ship when it caught fire. There were many injuries and the story made national news. He was the only fatality. As we were looking for his will, God showed me his passwords for his email account. I was able to share with the family some very important information and the passwords worked. And lastly, God came to me in a dream while I slept, he showed me that my husband's nephew had been shot. I immediately woke up and started praying at around 2:30 a.m. Brandon was in that dream showing me where he had been hurt. I saw 4 places, although later they would say it was 3 places. Brandon told me to tell his grandmom (my sister in law who was raising Brandon) that he was alright, tell her "Bye grandmom; love you!" But he just kept saying to me that he was alright. Because his death was mistaken identity, I told Bonnie every word and it helped her. Today, years later God still gives me messages for people including several who are Pastors now! While they were in the world, God told me that Roy, Otis, Beverly, and Gwen will preach. I was given very detailed messages for each one of them. Of course, they laughed and said NOT ME! All are preaching now. Sometimes we

7. BRIDGING GAPS: GOD'S GIFT TO ME

have to be bold and tread into unfamiliar territory for God to get the glory; not YOU!

Using my social media pages (Facebook and Instagram) I will tell people to leave their name and I will tell them very detailed things (not private things). I also give them clarity on the things going on in their life. Most people don't truly understand the gift of dreams or prophecy. But it gives clarity and it helps people to *Bridge their Gap and Embrace their Reality*. That is the name which I have chosen for my pages. I didn't understand at first what God was telling me when HE said, "You will help families, people, and strangers heal." But after all the positive testimonies, tears, and joy, I totally get it now.

8. DANCING FOR AN AUDIENCE OF ONE

DILEIKA WILSON-BALLARD

Before I grew in my relationship with the Lord I thought I was a good person. I was helpful, considerate, giving, and always sharing warm smiles with all I encountered. I didn't drink alcohol, never did any drugs, and never smoked cigarettes. Far from perfect, but striving to be good and helpful at all times. My vices were shoes, clothes, great tasting food, music and dancing.

My parents sent me for ballet lessons at a young age. I quickly discovered that I wanted to go straight to tap dancing which seemed fun and exciting. Unfortunately, I would have needed to take prerequisite classes before I could progress to tap and other genres of dance. So I rebelled until they withdrew me from the classes.

I have always loved dancing and music to include, reggae, reggaeton, soca, jazz, R&B, indie soul, and 80's music. I would dance anywhere and everywhere and would often sing out loud (and very off key). At around 19 years of age, I discovered night clubs. I would dance up a sweat and leave all my cares on that dance floor, usually arriving late and leaving when they were closing. I would say that dancing was my stress relief. I would shop for cute outfits and go out 3 -4 times a week. Dancing made me feel empowered, carefree, and fearless! I could be the only one on the dance floor and never feel self-conscious.

I grew up attending Baptist churches with my family. We attended church regularly and prayed together but I did not have a personal relationship with the Lord. I had an understanding of religion and what was expected of me. I never went to a church where I truly felt connected or a desire to serve. I didn't realize being a good person doing good things would never be enough to get me into heaven. Ephesians 2:8-9 makes that clear. It tells us, "For by grace you are saved through faith, and this is not from yourselves; it is God's gift – not from works, so that no one can boast. For we are His creation – created in Christ Jesus for good works, which God prepared ahead of time

8. DANCING FOR AN AUDIENCE OF ONE

so that we should walk in them." I would later gain that understanding as I matured in my spiritual walk.

While visiting a church in Maryland I saw my first praise dance. It was a group of teenage girls who danced passionately and cried after they danced. I remember thinking, "Wow, I love to dance, but it never made me cry." At that time, I was seeking a church home, but still had not yet developed a relationship with the Lord. I did not fully understand what I witnessed other than a beautiful dance to a beautiful song. A year later my cousin and her daughter performed a praise dance at a banquet during a woman's retreat. It was beautiful and anointed. Another cousin also performed a praise dance that evening; her dance and testimony were inspiring. I was still intrigued but still did not truly know what I was witnessing. My cousin and her daughter danced together at the banquet another year, and again I loved it but couldn't explain it.

Fast forward a few years. The Lord had healed me after a year-long battle with breast cancer. I finally finished my graduate degree and found myself separated from my husband of less than a year. I then moved to North Carolina to be near my family. I was feeling lost and overwhelmed by life. I was in my early 30's and had calmed down some; I was no longer going to the club 3 to 4 times a week. It had been a few years since I had stopped doing that. I was now only going out on Friday and Saturday nights. Dancing was still my stress relief.

I began to feel a pull to seek a relationship with the Lord. Instead of just going to the club every Friday and Saturday, I was now getting up Sunday mornings and visiting churches, looking for a church home. About a year into that journey I was invited to attend a service at New Hope Community Fellowship (NHCF) in Archdale, NC and I joined the church the third time I visited. I felt connected there, a small church with an awesome Pastor who both taught and preached, and, a beautiful and relatable First Lady. They had a warm and welcoming congregation that always made me feel like I was walking into a big hug, and they also had a praise dance every Sunday!

NHCF had 4 amazing dancers that alternated Sundays, and there was a praise dance toward the beginning of every service. They announced we would be doing a group praise dance for Easter and invited others in the congregation to participate. I felt a pull to the dance ministry but still did not know that it was a ministry. I was excited to join and loved attending practice after

8. DANCING FOR AN AUDIENCE OF ONE

church on Sunday's. When my purple and gold praise dance dress arrived, I was so excited! I felt official. I played the song on repeat in my car and practiced the dance over and over again.

On Resurrection Sunday we arrived early for one last practice and to have time to dress and get in position. I remember joking with some of the ladies as we were about to get lined up to go on the stage. I felt prepared and was hyped! We joined hands and prayed, thanking the Lord for the opportunity and asking that we decrease in ourselves so that we could increase in Him. That was when things first began to shift. I felt a stillness and a peace.

The music started, and we got into position. I remember feeling something fully coming over me. I couldn't see the person before me, or beside me. It was surreal. Everything and everyone around me faded away, I could barely hear the music. I felt transported to a beautiful place and I was dancing for an audience of One! The only One, The Great I Am! Every turn, every jump, every spin, every move was all for Him. It was overwhelming and beautiful! I don't remember leaving the stage, I don't remember anything other than the fact that I was crying. I tried to make sense of what happened, but I couldn't.

After that group dance, NHCF went back to the 4 being in rotation. I felt a pull to be more involved, so I joined the Usher Board and also began attending Bible Study. I was still going to the club on the weekends and attending church on Sunday. We did another group performance a few months later at a local outdoor festival. I was curious to see if I would have the same experience dancing outside as I did at church. It was even more amazing dancing before the Lord in the beauty of all He spoke into existence. I felt electrified and peaceful all at the same time. I remember going to my car after changing out of my praise dance dress to bask in that feeling. I wanted more!

A few months later, I had the opportunity to dance with the anointed dancer who led the NHCF praise dance team. We danced at the banquet of Women Walking in Faith, Growing in God annual retreat, the same retreat I saw my cousin and her daughter minister in dance. Again, I knew I was dancing before the Lord and I craved to have more of that experience. We danced the same song a few Sunday's later at NHCF. As I was added into the rotation at NHCF, I would be so filled with the Spirit that I often

8. DANCING FOR AN AUDIENCE OF ONE

found myself crying before I even started dancing. I am not the best dancer but I have a heart for the Lord and He uses me.

During that time, I was still going out to the club but it wasn't the same. No matter how good the DJ was, no matter how much I danced up a sweat, I couldn't replicate the amazing feeling I experienced when praise dancing. The Lord took away my appetite for that atmosphere and eventually that part of my life was phased out. I surrendered myself to dancing for the Lord. I learned that when I tried to dance in the flesh I wouldn't feel the Spirit overtake me. I learned the difference between dancing a song and ministering a song. I realized that I needed to first surrender totally to Him and when I did, He would bless me by allowing me to dance for Him.

I would sometimes hear other praise dancers grumble when they were called upon to minister in dance. I would always think, "How would they not want to dance before the Lord?" I love to minister in dance not for me to be in the spotlight, but for God to get all of the glory! It is truly not about me and that is what makes it so special. There are times when my feet are extremely swollen, or my back or knees hurt. I am thankful that He still graces me with the ability to minister in dance in spite of. My God is awesome!

Finding a church that I connected to with a true shepherd for a pastor and praise dancing have been instrumental in my spiritual growth. I received the gift of speaking in my holy language while at a praise dance conference. My passion for ministering in dance has led me to studying more of the Word. My pastor loves teaching and is an excellent teacher so I am able to study on my own and soak up all that he shares. I have grown tremendously in the last 7 years because of the refining process God is taking me through.

I love how the Lord communicates with me through music and dance. When I hear music, dance the lyrics in my head. My escape is now seeking Him. Where I once had a section of my closet for club clothes, I now have a section for my praise dance garments. *And David danced before the Lord with all his might (*2 Samuel 6:14) and I love to do so as well. Where I once had a craving to go out and dance up a sweat in night clubs, I now crave to be in His presence, to truly make Him my dwelling place. I am thankful for my relationship with the Lord.

8. DANCING FOR AN AUDIENCE OF ONE

I am thankful that I am continually growing in my relationship with Him! I am thankful for the blessing of being able to dance for my audience of One.

9. SURRENDER

AYESHIA DURU

I cannot recall the exact date I became a Christian. I was a teenager. After attending a church revival, I was convinced I was going to hell. At the time my family and I didn't regularly attend services together. Sometime later my mother, sisters and I started attending a local Baptist church. Obligation to my newly acquired religion led to a decision to become baptized. Memories can be foggy but it's one of my most salient reflections: baptism day. Dressed in white, head covered and waiting behind the pulpit to be called, I feared falling or drowning.

Off to college I went. It was an in-state college less than one hour away from home. During my college years, I occasionally attended an on-campus Bible study and church near campus. It was during Bible study I began processing my interpretations of Christianity and God.

The facilitator's name was Eric and he was one of the kindest people I knew. His spiritual convictions were confident and his relationship with God so sound. How did he achieve that?!

My experience with acute grief from losing my grandmother and best friend prompted anger and resentment toward God. I challenged Him with questions that have no answers; as painful events rarely do. In His kindness I encountered remnants of them both during my grieving period. Two different nights while silently weeping, my home was flooded with the smell of my grandmother's perfume and another the sound of smacking lips (I'd always chastise my friend for chewing with her mouth open because I would always hear the sound of her eating).

I would soon enter into a covenant with GOD through marriage; the beginning of an intimate relationship.

While in my sophomore year in college I became secretly engaged to a young man who was nicer than any boyfriend I previously had. I loved him and felt loved and cherished by him. During a service I attended with my fiancé and his father, I felt the pastor speaking directly to

9. SURRENDER

me about the importance of being in God's will. The ride home seemed longer than usual, and I asked God, "if this relationship is not your will, please make it clearly known." Overnight my fiancé suddenly became different in my eyes. He was suddenly undesirable and extremely annoying. I no longer found him attractive. Small odd things would evoke uncomfortable physical reactions in my body (nausea, headache, dizziness): the sound of him chewing, the music he listened to and the smell of his cologne (that I'd selected and loved). This left us both very confused. I'd later link my physical responses to my prayer. Ending our relationship was one of the hardest things I had done up to that day. Through tears, he pleaded with me to reconsider. He began asking what he'd done wrong while vowing to finish college if it'd make me happy. My response was that "we are going in different directions. A month after ending that relationship, I met my husband.

Our first date was a Sunday service and he cried from start to finish. My interpretation of those tears was that he and I connected spiritually to the Word that day.

What began as a friendship quickly became a deep soul connection and intense love. My husband has a complex background and bore heavy responsibilities. I sought God's counsel about our plans being His will. Asking is he "The One?" Since I did not encounter the same reactions the last time I asked Him this question, I said yes to his marriage proposal. During my junior year of college, we eloped.

A year after graduating we bought our first home and moved to the suburbs. I began attending a Nazarene church and first encountered a church community where people other than my mother, were developing their relationships with God and praying for and alongside me.

Our pastor was a great teacher. The biggest impact on me through his teachings was that God cares "who you become, not what you do." Until then, my questions revolved around works and those works would determine how God loved and accepted me. This was the underpinning of which I became to know who and what God is. LOVE.

Love is patient, love is kind, it does not envy, it does not boast, it is not proud. It does not dishonor others, it is not self-seeking, it is not easily angered, it keeps no record of wrongs.

1 Corinthians 13:4-5 (NIV).

9. SURRENDER

It is those words that I would be reminded of, by the Holy Spirit, when conflict, hurt, anger and disappointment surfaced in my marriage.

"I see you," I heard God say to me as I stood crying one day at the sink while inwardly asking if my husband saw all that I was doing. The honeymoon phase was in the past, we had a newborn and I worked over forty hours weekly. Exhaustion was my constant state and very likely I had some degree of postpartum depression. Four months after our first child was born, I was pregnant with our second child and was already feeling like a single parent because my husband was a consultant who travelled weekly. The opportunity to move to the Washington DC area was presented to my husband. It was exciting, the prospect of our family being together daily instead of the weekends, but the mere thought of moving caused me anxiety. Being a type A personality, I began researching housing, daycare and employment before my husband's offer was confirmed. Already stressed, becoming extraordinarily overwhelmed, I felt buried. Then the bouts of tears, mind racing insomnia and near paralyzing fear and worry burdened me daily.

One night something I had never experienced before occurred. Suddenly I was roused, without warning but couldn't open my eyes or move. Something was on my body weighing me down and I could not open my mouth. The more I tried to move the heavier the weight became. A thought surfaced so strongly, "if only you say the name of Jesus, whatever this is, it would leave." I'd stopped struggling but the weight became heavier along with my fear. The weight made it impossible to reach for my sleeping husband who was unaware of my struggle. Suddenly, I bit my tongue hard enough to draw blood, resulting in so much pain I was able to open my mouth and yell out "Jesus!" I sat up, barely able to breathe, with the taste of blood lingering in my mouth because the heaviness was gone. That was my first experience encountering the power in the name of Jesus and the Holy Spirit as counselor.

Florida, not Washington DC, became our new home which meant looking for a new church. While my entire family initially attended church together, by the time we relocated to Florida it was only my children and I. I had come to make peace with that fact. There was an inner struggle surrendering and submitting to my spouse as the head of my home. In my search for a new church home I found a non-denominational church. It was this church teaching that increased my interest and desire for God's

9. SURRENDER

word. There was a heavy emphasis on spiritual warfare, the third person of The Holy Trinity, and worship at this church. It was at this church my spirit was awakened to the tangible presence of God. It would be a common occurrence for the normal flow of service to be allowed to be interrupted. Prolonged singing, people kneeling in the aisles or lying in the back on the floor, the sound of weeping and praying in tongues and clapping were heard throughout the sanctuary. One particular service the pastor's wife was preaching and it felt as if she was looking and preaching directly to me. She said, "you are a healer." I remember at the moment smirking at the comment as my current health status was mediocre. I was on multiple medications and was in pain frequently. It was the way she looked at me when she said it that left me feeling uneasy. I had been praying for relief and healing from the frequent pain experienced. To hear someone say that I would heal people left me in disbelief. I shared this experience with a close friend and she said "healing comes in different forms, not just physical, you can speak the right words to an individual and it causes healing." Sometime later I dreamt and heard the same words, "You are a healer." This time the voice was the combination of wind, rushing water and the sound of a helicopter rotor blades spinning. I pondered that for a while and then shortly thereafter forgot the occurrences.

At a different service, I felt GOD was talking to me. "Do you have all the gifts God has promised," said the pastor. He was preaching on gifts of the Spirit. I so desperately wanted what he spoke of and if I'm honest, had believed previously that "those gifts" were only for *spiritual* Christians. By now in my Christian journey my mindset was beginning to shift. Believing, "if it's in the Bible, why not me?" Time and time again I responded to the altar call with church officials laying hands on me. I'd experienced nothing and was unable to speak in tongues when they commanded, until one night I was abruptly awakened with the need to pray. I was alone in my home as my family had recently relocated to a different state while I was waiting on licensure for a job. "Why am I awake, what do you need from me, what am I supposed to do," I asked God. That night as I lay on the floor singing and praying the gift of speaking in tongues manifested. "You're making that up. It's gibberish. Those words have no meaning." Over and over I heard these thoughts but because of my recent understanding of spiritual warfare was able to recognize them as lies from Satan. The season at this church helped me to encounter God as a faithful

9. SURRENDER

and giving Father. This scripture come to mind: Matthew 15:21-28.

The time came for us to move again. I felt a familiar uneasiness with starting over, but GOD had been so faithful in providing community that I wasn't afraid, at least about that need. Texas was our new home. A snare in what should have been an easy work transfer to a sister facility resulted in me working at a large teaching hospital with a long commute. Although I was grateful for employment, I was a bit resentful that I wasn't allowed to directly transfer into the local sister hospital. I thought, "really God, with all my experience?" It was during one of my long morning commutes that I experienced the peace described in Philippians 4:7. My mother in law had come to help with my children who were then 8 months, 4 and 5 years old. She offered to take my children back home with her so "I can rest." I politely declined stating that I was fine, inwardly saying they were *my* children. Simultaneously I had been praying for financial help. My morning commute either consisted of listening to praise and worship music or prayer. This particular morning, I felt the need for quiet. I was driving in silence when I heard God speak. I didn't hear audible words, more like an impression of a persistent thought. The answer to my prayer for financial help was sending my children to Nigeria with my mother in law. The dollar amount that we would spend on childcare as well as my past prayers for financial help surfaced to my conscious mind. My knee jerk reaction, "No way. I can't do that. But God, why in this way? You've seen where they would live!" I had visited my in-laws overseas and the conditions were not what I was accustomed to. My children would move to a place without constant electricity, running water or quality phone service. After praying more, I made what felt like an easy decision to send my children. Both my husband and mother-in-law were shocked by the decision but I just knew that they would be fine. First, we sent the youngest two children and then the oldest 6 months later.

I missed them while away but I was at peace. I never second guessed the decision. So many times I heard, "how could you do that?" God gave me peace, and it didn't make sense given their living conditions.

While working at that same hospital, I mistakenly received a text gossiping about me that was clearly meant for another coworker. When I called the person who sent it I asked what I'd done for her to speak about me in this manner. After profuse apologies I drove home seething. It's by grace there was not an accident. "Pray for her," I

9. SURRENDER

heard over and over again on my ride home. But I was too angry and hurt to immediately obey reminding God of the words she'd spoken against me and the disrespectful treatment I had received at work on multiple occasions. Again, I heard, "Pray!" In the way that only God can, after praying for her I saw her differently. I saw that her bitterness and anger was a mask for pain and insecurity. I saw that she was lonely and alone. God gave me new eyes to see my enemy. I now had a tangible definition of grace that I didn't have before. Did we ever become friends? No. But I no longer experienced strife and bitterness when going to work or disdain every time I saw her face. One year to the day I accepted the job at that facility, a position at the sister hospital I'd originally hoped to transfer to opened up. This time, although interviewed by the same management team, I was offered a position. I realized that God had a reason to send me to the first hospital, to learn to pray for my enemies. Since my move to Texas, God has met me when my spouse and I were separated physically and emotionally. Restoring love and compassion for each other and if I'm honest bringing us from the brink of divorce. He has humbled me, enabling me to ask for help from others when needing help financially and with my children. He has poured out blessings on me, giving me an opportunity to help others. He has rescued me from periods of sadness and fear, allowing me to hope and dream again. He carried me through an embarrassing bankruptcy having my wages garnished to buying and successfully operating a small business. I encounter God often; in the words of my children forgiving me when I've hurt them, in the face of my boss when disciplinary action could've been taken and wasn't, in hallways praying with tired and scared family members of those hospitalized, in the eyes of my spouse when he forgives me and with friends and family who love me. The more I ask for eyes to see and ears to hear those around me, the more I am confronted with opportunities to encounter God's love, grace and peace.

10. YOU ARE ENOUGH

SHERAE D. BELL

Prayer for the readers

Lord, I usher in Your Holy Spirit. I ask You to take control of my words, thoughts and emotions while speaking life into each person as they read this chapter. May the words leap from the page and take a lodging place in their hearts giving each of them a fresh anointing over their life. Lord. I ask you to give purpose to my words and let my words seal who you have called each of them to be and fulfill your calling on their life. May they grow stronger and not weary in their thoughts, with confirmation in their walk that you have not forgotten them. Place value in their very being validating that they are enough. I ask all these things in Jesus' name, Amen!

Thinking

When I think back over the many times that I have struggled with who I am, I always remember God telling me whose I am, then He reminds me of who He says that I am. There is no doubt that I am a woman, a wife, a mom, a grandmother, a sister and a friend. I could go on and on but those are just titles. Do they really identify me as a WOMAN of God who is sold out for Christ? Do those titles validate my value or my worth? Do they confirm that I am enough and will always be enough? Do those titles solidify that I am built for the race that God has prepared me for? No, they don't! Only God places value on my worthiness and solidifies my build.

As I sit here contemplating which encounter with God, I will elaborate on, all that keeps coming to my mind is that " I am enough". I have been chosen for such a time as this. A time that currently holds so much lack of surety on placing value on one's self that we are looking to everyone else for value. So many times, I have sat down to do something that I knew I could do and was called to do, but allowed the narrative of others to interfere. Their words and their thoughts of me would flow through my mind bringing my ability to trust God to a halt. I was allowing the words or the actions of others to determine

10. YOU ARE ENOUGH

my ability to walk boldly in the calling that ONLY God could and had placed on my life. People's thoughts and words had paralyzed my ability to speak God's words to others because I was beginning to doubt that it was Him who had called me. This was due to false prophecy that had no biblical backing but only personal agendas to destroy what God had already ordained. The words of others had me looking for validation that God had already given me in society's seasonal acceptance. I found myself crying out to God even more than before thinking that I was falling away, but the crying out was more of an indication that I was being drawn to Him in such a way that it was helping me to identify WHO He had truly called me to be. God had not forgotten me, nor had He invalidated who He declared that I was in my Mother's womb. Other's thoughts of me had now become my thoughts of myself. I often say "shut down the outside noise" but now I had to start shutting down the inside noise. The inside noise that had now bombarded my inner space and was continuously playing in my mind because I was beginning to believe what they were saying. It was no longer background noise but noise that was blurting out words of "not enough, you weren't made for this, you aren't called to this, leave this to the more qualified".

Words that did not equate to what I know God had whispered in my Mother's womb long before those negative words could even begin to take root and establish any type of space in the formation of my life. You see, our foundation is in Christ and because of this it is our guarantee that we are enough. It's not about who people believe we are but it's about who Christ says we are and how much belief we have in what He says.

"For you created my inmost being; you knit me together in my mother's womb. I praise you because I am fearfully and wonderfully made; your works are wonderful; I know that full well. My frame was not hidden from you when I was made in the secret place, when I was woven together in the depths of the earth. Your eyes saw my unformed body; all the days ordained for me were written in your book before one of them came to be. How precious to me are your thoughts, God! How vast is the sum of them! Were I to count them, they would outnumber the grains of sand when I awake, I am still with you." Psalm 139:13-18 (NIV)

Revealing

God was revealing to me that it wasn't outsiders tearing me apart; it was the ME within that was tearing me apart. How could I walk daily in His WORD, with Him

10. YOU ARE ENOUGH

but not trust Him in the wake of the process? How could I allow people that did not know my innermost thoughts or struggles determine my outermost actions? How could I allow those that did not spend alone time with me to dictate what my revealing time would look like? It was "ME" that was not believing what I knew God was saying about me because I was not trusting the process. As my husband once told me, I needed to embrace who God called me to be, declare who God called me to be and then watch God bring it to pass who He had called me to be. If I had not yet believed that I was enough how could I expect others to believe and entrust in my calling? If I was not willing to step out on FAITH and walk boldly in my calling, why should I expect others to understand that I had been called? If I was not going to continue to seek and embrace God in every process of my journey how did I expect to get to my ordained destination? I had to come to the realization of what it meant by God being sovereign. I had to understand and truly believe that God was the ruler over everything that I had and would encounter in my life. I had to recognize that this world that I live in could not interfere with God's determination that I was enough to fulfill His purpose and that I was worthy of everything that He had whispered in my mother's womb about me. I had to stop pitying myself for every little pothole that I fell into, every bump that I had hit and every step that I had missed and understand that those are the ingredients to making me ENOUGH. These were the obstacles that made me stronger and able to forgive others for all that they said or had done to deter me from the predestined journey that had been paved for me by my heavenly Father. God had already put HIS STAMP of APPROVAL on me, but I would not let the ink dry before I would begin to flaunt who He had called me to be, not embracing my strengths and weaknesses in their totality. God was constantly reminding me that there was nothing lacking, missing or broken in me, I just needed to embrace my flaws because my flaws are where my beauty lies. In Isaiah 61:3, His WORD says that He would give me BEAUTY for my ashes but in order to receive the BEAUTY, I had to continue through the burning process to receive the promise of the Beauty. But, instead I was seeing my weaknesses as brokenness not realizing that this is where my ministry was being birthed. You see, I don't believe I can minister from a place that I have never been, but I must also understand that to be effective in my ministry, I must push through and not reside in that place of pain. All the hurt, the negativity, the fear and the pain was strengthening me to speak life into others and walk in my divine appointment. Not forsaking anything that I had gone through but understanding that I was enough from the beginning to the end. That God had established my value and I needed to realize that I was worthy of the calling that He had placed on my life.

Accepting

I am so glad that God is a loving God and has so much love for me that His love covers all my sins.

"Above all, love each other deeply, because love covers over a multitude of sins." - 1ˢᵗ Peter 4:8

The enemy would love to make us relive our wrongdoings daily by trying to remind us of what we have done and use our sins against us.

"The steadfast love of the LORD never ceases; his mercies never come to an end; they are new every morning; great is your faithfulness." - Lamentations 3:22-23 (ESV)

So, remember the next time that someone or the voice within tells you that you are not enough, don't hesitate to reflect on the scriptures and pray them back to God. For He is not man therefore HE cannot lie. Jesus came to give us an abundant life. How we use that life is a choice of ours. What we believe will dictate who we become. Who we become will identify who we trust. Who we trust will define our worth. And finally, our worth will validate that we are enough. We must remember that no one other than the Father can place worthiness on us and that was done when HE died on the cross for US. He said at that very moment that it was FINISHED. We were created to be WHOLE. In order to understand your worth and to know that you are enough you must first understand and know the Creator Himself.

Lord, I ask You to speak life into our existence and open our hearts, so we can feel Your presence and live out the value that you have placed on us. The value you have placed on us is greater than anything that our minds could ever comprehend. Remove the darkness from our eyes so we can walk into the glory of your light. Give us ears to hear so that when silence comes, we will reflect on your spoken WORD in the midst of our thoughts. Let us know that we will NEVER walk alone and give us peace and comfort so we will not retreat to our own thoughts of discouragement. Lord, move in us and for us as You see fit. Keep us focused on our desire to live for You and not listen to the outside noise or quiet whispers of our mind trying to hinder us as we step out in faith.

10. YOU ARE ENOUGH

Remind us of who you say we are and who we belong to, so that we will not hesitate as You show us Your will for our lives, in Jesus's name, AMEN!

11. SWEET MAGNOLIA'S BIBLE

Sharon Finney

Thirty-two years have passed. I continue to miss my mother's physical presence, but I am blessed by sweet reminders of her in my thoughts, dreams, and occasionally in a random activity. This one particular moment from December 2019 really took me by surprise.

One morning, I reached in a drawer that I don't open on a daily basis. I was searching for something and ran across mom's bible. An inspirational note was taped to the inside of this bible. On the next page was her name and the date as written so neatly by mom. It was December 12, 1964.

She was an avid reader, so this Bible was always on her nightstand for early reading and nightly meditation. It has been in my possession ever since packing up her things in late 1988, months after her passing. Imagine my surprise when I grabbed my phone and verified the date. It was the morning of December 12th. Mom wrote in that bible exactly 55 years ago from when I randomly reached for it. Whenever I lay hands on her bible, I smile. But my smile on that morning was extra special because God sent her my way and even included a message that I needed at the moment. I share this with you because someone else needs to know just how powerful God is. You can be comforted not just in troubling times but even when things are relatively smooth.

The scripture that comes to mind is John 14:16. *And I will ask the Father, and he will give you another advocate to help you and be with you forever.* (NIV).

When I shared this special moment on my social media pages, I stated that my mother stopped by for a visit that December morning. I don't know who else might have seen it my way or believed it, but that is how I felt in the moment. I still thank God daily for my Sweet Magnolia.

MEET THE VISIONARY AUTHOR

SHARON FINNEY

Sharon Finney is an Army veteran on a mission to encourage and inspire through writing, for growth and healing. She is the author of the memoir, Sweet Magnolia and has co-authored three projects between 2017 and 2019 with Lila Holley (Camouflaged Sisters) and Shirley LaTour (Out of the Shadows Outreach Ministry) all of which are Amazon best sellers. After publishing Sweet Magnolia, Sharon established the Magnolia M. Bradford Memorial Scholarship as a tribute to her late mother. Book sales helped to fund the 2018 scholarship. Encounters with God is the first project released by her new company, Rose of Sharon Publishing.

In addition to writing, Sharon is passionate about healthy marriages. In 2012, she earned a Master of Arts in Human Services, specializing in Marriage & Family Counseling. She later started L&S Enterprise, LLC with her husband, Rev. Lewis H. Finney. Their company provides Christian-based premarital counseling and marriage enrichment services. Sharon is on the ministerial team at Christlike Ministries: A Church Without Walls 2. She is a devoted wife, mother and grandmother who enjoys traveling, spending time with family and supporting charitable endeavors in her local community.

Learn more:

Email: authorsharonfinney@gmail.com

Website: sharonfinney.com

Instagram: @authorsharonfinney

MEET THE COAUTHORS

APRIL JOY BOWDEN

April Joy was raised in Richmond, VA. Separated from her older siblings after the passing of her mother, April's love for writing began in the form of exchanging letters. She knew at an early age that she wanted to share her joy of writing with others with a dream of having a book published. Her childhood dream was achieved, and this collaboration marks her third completed book.

When April is not writing, she enjoys logging miles on the pavement and interacting with participants of her fitness page @IRUNTHISC1TY. She also enjoys cooking, planning events and learning about new and exciting products with her Mary Kay business.

April currently splits her time living in North Carolina and Virginia. She works as a photographer and in various programs with the goal of enriching the lives of our youth.

Connect with April via Facebook under the username Author April Joy Bowden and on Instagram under the name Author AprilJoy.

AYESHIA DURU

Ayeshia Duru practices as a clinical pharmacist at a local hospital in Plano, Texas. She co-owns and operates a bubble tea business with her husband but what she is most passionate about is changing the lives of women. As a coach her mission is to teach and encourage women how to treasure themselves by changing what they put into their bodies and their minds. Her mission: connecting women on a journey towards discovering the fullness of God's grace, their worth and true authentic self. Her vision: a community of women who love lavishly and live authentically thereby changing those they encounter. She has appeared as a freelance writer in the online magazine *Digest This! Ministry Magazine.*. She enjoys taking long walks, watching movies and playing board games with her young adult children 13, 17 and 18 years old. Learning how to love and come alongside her husband Chimezie Duru of 22 years as his helpmate is what she is most proud of.

Contact Ayeshia at authorayeshiaduru@gmail.com

Facebook: @authorayeshiaduru

DEBLEN B. EDGE

Deblen Edge was born in North Carolina and graduated from high school in June 1972. She later moved to the New York/New Jersey area where she lived for several years. After enlisting in the United States Air Force in 1978, her life was filled with travels to places such as Japan, Korea, Germany, Belgium, England, Turkey, France and Honduras as well as several states. After her 22 years of adventures, she retired from the United States Air Force as a Master Sergeant in December 1999. Upon her retirement she worked as a Federal Contractor and a Federal employee. Currently,

DEBLEN B. EDGE

Deblen is completely retired and lives in Maryland. Deblen is very active in her church and community. Her focus is on volunteering her time to assist with veterans, special Women Veteran programs and organizations.

Contact Deblen at dege50@comcast.net

DILEIKA WILSON-BALLARD

Dileika Wilson-Ballard is married to Minister Timothy Oneal Ballard and they are the proud parents of their fur baby, a shih tzu, Halo Sophia. She earned her Master's in Human Resource Management from the Catholic University of America. Dileika co-owns Timeless Wigs and Marvelous Things in downtown Salisbury, NC, with her mother, Marva Wilson and she is a 10 year and counting breast cancer survivor.

Dileika attends New Hope Community Fellowship in Archdale, NC under Pastor Lee Bynum where she serves in their praise dance ministry, New Hope In Motion, and she serves as an usher. She has a passion for helping others and actively serves her community as a board member on a non-profit board. Her favorite quote is "I would rather have my worst day with the Lord than my best day without Him" and her favorite scripture is Proverbs 31:25.

Contact Dileika at: timelesswmt@gmail.com

DONNA SUTTLES

Donna "DeeDee" Suttles is a writer, poet and Spiritual Prophetess. She has copy-written two books of poetry. She is the founder of *Bridging Gaps Embracing Reality*. This online podcast addresses modern-day concerns of her viewership while providing spiritual direction and guidance.

Donna has been married to Daniel, for more than 32 years. They have two adult children, Danielle and Daniel who she truly cherishes along with her father Mr. William D. Tolson and bonus mom Desiree and especially her siblings. Praise God!

In her spare time, she loves to travel, and she immerses herself in God's Word to edify, enlighten and inform God's people. She uses her gift to provide joy, happiness and closure. Donna unlocks the hurt and pain to allow believers to bridge their own gaps to embrace reality. Most importantly, she glorifies Jesus and leads souls back to Christ.

Contact Donna Suttles at deedeesutt@yahoo.com

MARVA J. CUMBERBATCH WILSON

Rev. **Marva J. Cumberbatch-Wilson** is an ordained minister of the gospel of Jesus Christ, and the Founder / Director of *Women Walking In Faith Growing In God Ministry*. She is also Co-owner of Timeless Wigs and Marvelous Things in Salisbury, North Carolina. She is Married to Dr. Dennis Wilson, and they are the blessed parents of three adult children: Jessica, Dileika, Dennis II; three grandchildren: Angelica, Hector, Sydney; and one fur-gran-dog: Halo Sophia. Marva is an honor graduate of Shaw University, North Carolina, and also a graduate of LeeWard Community College, Hawaii. She is a leader, teacher, mentor, encourager, prayer warrior, and overcomer. Marva is a member of New Hope Community Fellowship Church, Archdale, North Carolina. Two of her favorite scriptures are: 2 Corinthians 5:7, and Hebrews 11:1-6.

Contact Rev. Wilson by email at

Alwayswalkinginfaith@gmail.com

SHERAE D. BELL

Sherae **D. Bell** is a licensed Minister, Author and Inspirational Speaker. She is the founder of "Affirmed Ministries" and "Sherae Speaks". Originally from Baltimore City, she attended Baltimore City College HS and Morgan State University. She honorably served 6 years in the Army Reserves. Sherae has a passion and a calling to see women delivered and set free from the captivity of their past. She lives out her motto, 'From a past of shame to a future of deliverance.' She has been blessed to speak to women's groups across the country and is amazed by how God uses her trials and tribulations to build her ministry's platform. Her love for running has helped her Mentor for 'Girls on The Run' and hosts a Sunday morning women's running group. She also enjoys spending time with her family and drawing. Currently, she resides in Leesburg, VA, with her husband, James and dog, Zori. Sherae has two children and 3 grandchildren.

For Booking or retail purchases:

Sherae Bell

Website: www.sheraebell.com

Email: sheraespeaks@sheraebell.com

Phone: 571.252.9413

TAMICA R. SIMON

Tamica Simon is a Navy veteran residing in Philadelphia, Pennsylvania and working in healthcare. She loves history and travel and has visited the ancient city of Ephesus, House of the Virgin Mary, Basilica of St. John, Grotto of St. Paul, Golden Altar of San Jose Church, Lima Cathedral and Monastery de San Francisco. She also enjoys exploring details of the slave trade and has visited ports and museums in Ghana, Guadeloupe, Puerto Rico and Tanzania. She has a Psychology degree from St Leo University and Master of

Business Administration and Health Administration from Drexel University.

Tamica is the mother of two and grandmother of four unless you include the granddog. Her travels have led her to the love of her life and while much of her writing is done on beaches, balconies, and long flights, she will soon add another location to the list.

Email: AuthorTamica@gmail.com

Website: Melanatedmigration.com

Instagram: @melanatedmigration

VERNETTA DUNBAR

Vernetta **Wood Dunbar** is a minister, wife, and mother of five children. She is a Philadelphia native currently residing in Neptune, NJ. Vernetta is the founder of Sacred Heart Ministry, where the mission is to be a vessel to change one life at a time. She is the author and publisher of *Digest This! Ministry Magazine*. Her ministry has reached many including those living in Africa, Philippines and some parts of Europe. Vernetta is a Certified Professional Coder; she currently manages two departments, Coding/Charge Entry, and AR for a Gastroenterology MSO. An entrepreneur at heart, she co owns Doris Jean Catering with her husband Tracy and Mani's Hair Supply with her daughter Imani. Vernetta has a heart for God and is extremely grateful for the opportunity to serve.

Learn more by email: sacredheartministry@aol.com

Websites: magcloud.com *Digest This! Ministry Magazine* and www.touchedbymani.com

Facebook: Sacred Heart Ministry

Instagram: @sacredheartmin

eBook and Paperback available on Amazon!
Amazon.com/author/sharonfinney

L&S Enterprise, LLC
Marriage Enrichment and **Premarital Counseling**
from a Christian perspective.
www.LSEnterprise.org

Visit sharonfinney.com to learn more about Rose of Sharon Publishing.

Shawn

Thank you for your support. 1992 seems like yesterday on some days and like an eternity ago on others. Happy to have you as more than a college memory.

Blessings to you JB

One page
One sip at a time
Enjoy!

April

Made in the USA
Middletown, DE
03 November 2020